Cleo, Camping, Emmar

Filming's not as glamorous as it's cracked up to be. It's a bit of a miserable business if your caravan leaks, your co-star's a manic depressive, and those younger women aren't as young as they used to be.

Carrying on in the great tradition of British comedy, *Cleo, Camping, Emmanuelle and Dick* takes some familiar faces and gets a bit familiar with them.

Terry Johnson's plays include *Amabel* (Bush, London, 1979); *Days Here So Dark* (Paines Plough at the Tricycle, London, 1981); *Insignificance* (Royal Court, London, 1982 and filmed by Nicolas Roeg, 1985); *Cries from the Mammal House* (Open Heart Enterprises with the Royal Court, London, 1984); *Unsuitable for Adults* (Bush, London, 1984); *Tuesday's Child*, written with Kate Lock (Theatre Royal, Stratford East, 1985); *Imagine Drowning* (Hampstead Theatre, London, 1991); *Hysteria* (Royal Court, London, 1993; Duke of York's Theatre as part of the Royal Court Classics season, 1995); *Dead Funny* (Hampstead Theatre, 1994); an adaptation of Edward Ravenscroft's *The London Cuckolds* (Royal National Theatre, 1998) and *The Graduate*, an adaptation from the novel and film script (Gielgud Theatre, 2000, and Broadway, 2002).

by the same author

Terry Johnson Plays: 1
(Insignificance, Unsuitable for Adults, Cries from the
Mammal House)

Terry Johnson Plays: 2
(Imagine Drowning, Hysteria, Dead Funny)

Dead Funny
Hysteria
Imagine Drowning
The London Cuckolds

for a complete catalogue of Methuen write to:

Methuen Publishing Limited
20 Vauxhall Bridge Road
London SW1V 2SA

Cleo, Camping, Emmanuelle and Dick

(Cor, Blimey!)

Terry Johnson

Methuen Drama

First published in Great Britain in 1998
by Methuen Publishing Limited

This revised edition published in 2002.

1 3 5 7 9 10 8 6 4 2

Methuen Publishing Ltd
215 Vauxhall Bridge Road, London SW1V 1EJ

Copyright © 1998 by Terry Johnson
The right of Terry Johnson to be identified as the author of this
work has been asserted by him in accordance with the Copyright,
Designs and Patents Act, 1988

Methuen Publishing UK Limited Reg. No. 3543167

A CIP catalogue record for this book
is available from the British Library

Papers used by Methuen Publishing Limited are natural, recyclable products
made from wood grown in sustainable forests. The manufacturing processes
conform to the environmental regulations of the country of origin.

ISBN 0 413 73500 1

Typeset by Deltatype Ltd, Birkenhead, Merseyside
Printed and bound in Great Britain by
Mackays of Chatham PLC, Chatham, Kent

Caution

All rights whatsoever in this play are strictly reserved and application
for performance etc. should be made before rehearsals begin to
Leah Schmidt, The Agency (London) Ltd, 24 Pottery Lane, Holland Park,
London W11 4LZ. No performance may be given unless a
licence has been obtained.

Cleo, Camping, Emmanuelle
and Dick

Cleo, Camping, Emmanuelle and Dick was first performed in the Lyttelton auditorium of the Royal National Theatre on 4 September 1998. The cast was as follows:

Sid	Geoffrey Hutchings
Kenneth	Adam Godley
Barbara	Samantha Spiro
Sally	Jacqueline Defferary
Imogen	Gina Bellman
Eddie	Kenneth MacDonald

Directed by Terry Johnson
Designed by William Dudley
Lighting by Simon Corder
Costumes by Nettie Edwards
Music by Barrington Pheloung
Sound by Adam Rudd

Characters

Sid, *forty, eventually late fifties.*
Kenneth, *late thirties, eventually early fifties.*
Barbara, *twenty-five, eventually late thirties.*
Sally, *eighteen, eventually mid-thirties. Petite, intense, in denial of herself.*
Imogen, *nineteen, eventually late twenties. Attractive.*
Eddie, *early thirties / late thirties. Huge East-Ender.*

Setting

A caravan, circa early sixties.

Act One

Cleo. 1964.

A spanking new caravan with all mod cons, including shower and toilet. A telephone line comes in through the window. Beyond, the austere prison camp walls of the Pinewood Studio buildings.

*Enter **Sally**, eighteen years old. She takes off her coat, drops her large bag, and looks around her. Sees a pile of a man's clothing and sets about tidying. Hanging the trousers she breaks off to smell the jacket, imagining the man. Then hesitates to pick up the crumpled underwear. Uses two fingers and holds the pants at arm's length. Enter **Sid**, broad-featured, big-nosed, about forty years old, costumed as Mark Antony.*

Sid Afternoon.

Sally Oh, hello.

Sid If you want to fiddle about with my pants I'd be very grateful if you'd wait 'til I've got them on.

Sally Sorry.

She offers them to him.

Sid I don't want them; I know where they've been.

She puts the pants on the table.

Burning question is: where have *you* been?

Sally What?

Sid All my life.

Sally Um . . .

Sid I wish I'd met you sooner; a girl with your fearless attitude to underwear.

Sally I'm Sally.

Sid Saluté.

Sally   Pardon?

Sid   That's Shakespeare that is. That's Roman for 'Hello sweetheart'. I'm giving me Mark Antony.

Sally   I know. I'm your new dresser?

Sid   You'll be seeing a lot of me, then.

Sally   Oh . . . probably.

Sid   Definitely. You're in the nick of time too.

Sally   Am I?

Sid   There's a rip in me toga.

Sally   Oh, whoops.

Sid   Second-hand tat.

Sally   I'll take it to wardrobe, shall I?

Sid   No, it's not that bad. Just put a safety pin in it or something.

Sally   Right.

She rummages in her bag. He drinks some bourbon and dials the phone.

Sid   Long as it fits. I'm not a silk purse sort of performer. I'm more at home in a pig's ear.

She kneels in front of him to tack-stitch the skirt.

Sid   (*phone*)   Freddie? Sid. I missed the third at Aintree, mate; check my accumulator, will you? What's a nice girl like you doing in a place like that?

Sally   Oh, it's Richard Burton's.

Sid   Is it? I've been using it for years.

Sally   The toga. Gwenda just said; she got a job-lot off *Cleopatra*. He probably tore this fending off the Egyptians.

Sid   Fending off the missus, more like. (*Phone.*) Freddie? Oh for fu . . . crying out loud. I'm going to take a contract out on that bloody Edridge. Do me a shilling each way on Twice Nightly, will you?

Sally It could do with a good clean, I know that.

Sid I beg your pardon?

Sally The toga.

Sid (*phone*) You what? Oh come on, Freddie; it's only a couple of bob. All right, all right. I'll send the girl round with it. Well, half an hour; she's got her hands full at the moment. Freddie, you're a gent. Whose missus, my missus? What did you tell her? Good thinking. I'll catch you later.

Puts the phone down.

While you're down there, could you do us a favour?

Sally I've only got two hands.

Sid So what's the problem?

Sally *stops, embarrassed.*

Sid That's a lovely shade of pink. I could live with that.

Sally I was warned about you.

Sid Lies. All lies.

Sally I took the job anyway because I was quite intrigued.

Sid All true then. Every word of it.

Sally I'm disappointed.

Sid Vicious falsehoods, unfounded fabrications, vile, malicious rumours . . .

She bites the thread.

Whoop . . .

Sally Finished.

Sid One blinding moment there I'd have put five grand on the existence of God.

Sally   I'm your third dresser since Monday, aren't I?

Sid   I've been the victim of a strange lesbian conspiracy. I hope you're not one of them.

Sally   No, I'm not.

Sid   How'd you get the job then?

Sally   I wrote to the studios? Got the usual 'we'll put you on file'. I never really dreamed I'd really be here.

Sid   It's not that surprising. I seem to get through dozens of you.

Sally   Production office gave me your mail.

Sid   Dump it. Have you got a boyfriend?

Sally   Um . . . no.

Sid   Do you live on your own?

Sally   I live with my mum.

Sid   That's lovely. How is she?

Sally   Dead. Um . . . she died. (*She laughs a little hysterical laugh.*) She died in April. I'm sorry. I live on my own.

Sid   What about your dad?

Sally   My dad?

Sid   Your dad.

Sally   I don't know my dad.

Sid   That's a shame.

Sally   What should I do with this?

Sid   Oh, just chuck it away. (*Phone.*) Bernie? Sid. Can you lend me fifty quid? Don't get philosophical about it; I want to get a little present for Val and I've left me wallet at home. Good man. I'll send the new girl over. *Arrivederci.*

Puts down the phone.

Sally   You want me to just . . . throw it away?

Sid That's right. Now I need you to get fifty quid off Bernie in dressing-room six and give Jim in number two the thirty I owe him.

Sally Don't you read your fan mail?

Sid Never; it's all from mad people. Then nip the twenty round to the Plough. Look for a blimp on a bar-stool.

Sally And give him two shillings?

Sid Give him the twenty.

Sally Mmm?

Sid Ten quid's a shilling. Two and six is twenty-five quid. Give him a couple of bob.

Sally Twenty pounds.

Sid Bright girl. Get going.

Sally I don't think this is in my job description.

Sid It's very short, your job description. Three words. Keep. Sid. Happy. That's not difficult to understand unless you're a lesbian.

Sally I'm not a lesbian.

Sid What are you doing tomorrow night, then?

Sally Nothing. I mean no. Don't.

Sid I'll never understand women your age. When I was *your* age I never understood women your age. Now I'm *my* age I don't understand women any age. Do you play poker?

Sally Have done, why?

Sid It whiles away the hours.

Sally I'd better get your bet on.

Sid No hurry. Freddie gets a bit jumpy, but he always lays the bet.

Sally You gamble a lot?

Sid   Naaah.

Sally   What about the poker?

Sid   That's not for money. That's for fun. C'mon; couple of hands.

Sally   I'm supposed to be working.

Sid   Uh, uh; Keep Sid Happy.

Sally   But I've got this list of things to do.

Sid   You're probably right. We'd barely get started. Well, not barely enough, anyway.

Sally   Pardon?

Sid   Nothing.

Sally   I'd better get on then.

Sid *can't let her go.*

Sid   Would you like one of these?

Sally   What is it?

Sid   Passion fruit.

Sally   Looks horrible.

Sid   It's tropical. You can only get these down Covent Garden. Very exotic. Go on; have a taste.

Sally   No thanks.

Sid   You want to live for ever? Go on.

Sally   Oh, all right. If you insist.

Sid   Careful.

Sally   Ooh. Whoops.

Sid   Not like that.

Sally   All down my chin.

Sid   Here; let me show you. You can't just bite into it because the skin is very bitter. The flesh on the other hand is very sweet. So before you can eat you have to make a little incision like this, then open it up like this . . . there you go.

Sally Oh.

Sid Nice?

Sally Lovely. Mmm. That is nice.

Sid *wipes a drip from her chin with his finger and tastes it.*

Sally It's true, isn't it?

Sid What about?

Sally You.

Sid Every word. Especially the rumours. You going to give us a kiss then?

Sally I've only just walked through the door.

Sid And I bless the moment. It's the watching you walk out again I'm having trouble with.

Sally Well, I'll be back.

Sid Not necessarily. Some of you I never see again.

Sally Are you surprised?

Sid I'll tell you what; give us a kiss and then we decide what sort of kiss it was. Quick hello, long goodbye, or the first of a few.

Sally Yes, but then what?

Sid But what but then what?

Sally You have to think about the consequences.

Sid I was. I do. I am.

Sally No, but it's not . . .

Sid What?

Sally Just don't.

Sid   I can't help it. It's something about that little bit right there.

Sally   Stop it.

Sid   Shadowy little curve just there.

Sally   Don't.

Sid   Why not?

Sally   Because you mustn't.

Sid leans forward to kiss her. Enter **Kenneth**, *taller than* **Sid**, *fine-featured, aquiline nose, dressed as Julius Caesar.*

Kenneth   This is an absolute disgrace.

Sid   Gawd strewth.

Kenneth   I don't mind telling you I am OUTRAGED.

Sid   Gawd strewth.

Kenneth   I have been hostage to this bloody profession for more years than I care to remember but this takes the biscuit, this does. And I'm not talking your common old Rich Tea. I'm not talking mere Custard Cream. I am talking your full Garibaldi!

Sid   Don't bother to knock.

Kenneth   If I bothered to knock every time there was a danger of finding you *in flagrante* with some witless polony I'd have the door off its hinges.

Sally   We weren't doing anything.

Kenneth   Well, it's a first, dearie. You half his age and both of you vertical.

Sid   Keep your filthy innuendos to yourself.

Kenneth   Well then, you keep *your* filthy in-your-end-os off the unit.

Laughs like a machine-gun.

Sid   There's a lady present, shut your gob.

Sally I'll see you later.

Sid No, no, no. You stay put. You shove off.

Kenneth No, I've got a bone to pick with you. And I'm not talking clavicle, I'm not talking metacarpal here, I'm talking ilium and scapula. I'm talking the sort of bone you give a Rottweiler and NEVER GET BACK. I don't know who you are but I'm sure you've got better things to do than stand there gawping at me.

Sid She's not gawping at anyone.

Kenneth *flashes* **Sally**.

Sally Oh.

Kenneth Didn't see that then, did she?

Sally Excuse me.

Exit **Sally**.

Sid I'll see you later, sweetheart. You know what you are?

Kenneth Completely disinterested in your opinion, for a start. You should know I've spoken to my agent, I shall speak to Peter at the wrap and I shall scream blue murder at Gerald the next time I vada his 'orrible eek. First A.D. said it was a tatty old caravan and more fool you but it's not, is it? This is not a tatty old caravan, this is a Merry Traveller.

Sid Correct.

Kenneth It's a Merry fucking Traveller.

Sid It's *my* Merry Traveller.

Kenneth That dressing-room block is falling to bits.

Sid I know.

Kenneth It's damp, it's drafty, the plaster's coming off the walls . . .

Sid I know.

Kenneth   And there's no hot water!

Sid   Piping hot in here, mate. Ascot boiler, TV, all mod cons.

Kenneth   There's a Nubian handmaiden just sprained her ankle trying to get her black off in the sink.

Sid   Coloured boyfriend?

Kenneth   Yes, and that's about as witty as it gets with you, isn't it? Peurile double entendres.

Sid   That's twice as witty as a single entendre, mate, which is more your mark.

Sid *phones.*

Kenneth   And that's a toilet. There's me 'olding it in all day and they've given you your own toilet. What have you ever done to deserve a toilet? Stupid question.

Sid (*phone*)   Supporting Artists, mate.

Kenneth   And you've got a shower.

Sid (*phone*)   Female, you twit.

Kenneth   They've given a shower to a man whose idea of personal hygiene is opening the window a snidge. This is an absolute disgrace. This is my *ninth*.

Sid   This is *my* ninth.

Kenneth   I was in the first. I was in *Constable*.

Sid   I was in *Cabby*.

Kenneth   *Cabby* was unadulterated shite.

Sid   I see; if I'm in it and you're not, it's shite.

Kenneth   Perfectly reasonable supposition.

Sid (*phone*)   Hello, it's Sidney. Hello, poppet. I hear there's a Nubian slave in a bit of trouble. Hand her the phone, will you?

Kenneth   And how much are you on?

Sid I knew that was coming.

Kenneth I'm no longer prepared to prostitute my incandescent talent to this unspeakable tat if it's no longer favoured nations. Working for a pittance is only bearable if you're working for a pittance too.

Sid They've always treated me very nicely. (*Phone.*) Hello, sweetheart, this is Sidney. I hear you're having trouble with your ablutions.

Kenneth Hawtrey's so incensed he almost sobered up.

Sid (*phone*) I know, it's a right pit; that's why I've got my own facilities which include a Super Spa shower unit which is entirely at your disposal.

Kenneth She's not that daft.

Sid Right then. See you in a couple of minutes.

Kenneth You know it's a short step from seducing the walk-ons to eating the props.

Sid Never bothered me, mate; I hate to see either go to waste.

Kenneth Don't think I don't know what you want this for.

Sid Bit of peace and quiet as befits the temperament of a creative artiste.

Kenneth Creative artiste? There's only one thing you ever create which is probably why they've given you the toilet. I know what you want this for.

Sid Do us a favour and fall on your dagger.

Kenneth There'll come a lunchtime you'll be busy in here, I'll pull your wheelchocks out and you'll bounce all the way to Sound Stage Four.

Sid I watched the rough cut of *Spying*.

Kenneth Yes?

Sid   That new girl. The blonde.

Kenneth   You'd be so lucky.

Sid   She seemed like a nice girl.

Kenneth   I thought *Spying* reached a level of cinematic sophistication hitherto unwitnessed in this neck of the woods. A sort of farce-noir, I thought. A genuine 'omage. And some real comic chemistry between the characters for once. What did you think?

Sid   I wasn't in it.

Kenneth   We noticed.

Sid   What's she like? The new girl?

Kenneth   Fluffed her first line. I made some vaguely caustic remark and she gave me a right bleeding mouthful. When we did the snog she said me beard was like Fenella's minge. I was quite taken with her.

Sid   She's got a lovely screen presence. Very good on camera. Very good delivery, good diction. Intelligent interpretation. And the sort of backside you can put your beer on as you walk past.

Kenneth   I'm sure I wouldn't know.

Sid   She'd have *you* beat in a mincing contest, mate. More's the bleeding miracle. How was the snog?

Kenneth   Well, I wouldn't confide this to a reprobate like you were it not bound to frustrate you beyond all reason, but from a purely objective point of view she was a good enough kisser to give me the half-hard.

Sid   You're joking.

Kenneth   Yes, the perverse pneumatics of desire never cease to astonish. Hasn't happened to me since Jim Dale went down the stairs on that hospital trolley.

Sid   Is she fixed?

Kenneth   She's getting married on Saturday.

Sid   What's today?

Kenneth   Thursday.

Sid   That's a bit tight.

Kenneth   Even for you.

Sid   Have you got her number?

Kenneth   Why would I want her number?

Sid   Those knockers. Man to man, or near-as-damn-it, are they real?

Kenneth   How's your wife, Sidney?

Sid   She's fine.

Kenneth   Doesn't it strike you in the least bit hypocritical, posing as a devoted family man whilst incessantly propositioning these poor girls?

Sid   Not my fault, mate; long as they keep giving me the Romantic lead, I'll keep doing the research.

Someone knocks on the door.

Imogen   Hello?

Sid   Now make yourself scarce. *Entrez-vous.*

Enter **Imogen**. *Tall, attractive, half blacked-up.*

Sid   Step right up.

Imogen   Hello.

Sid   Watch your step there; it's a bit perilous.

Kenneth   Yes, you can say that again. Leave your knickers at the door if you're coming in here, dearie.

Imogen   I'm Imo.

Sid   I'm Sidney.

Imogen   Hello.

Sid   This is Kenneth; he was about to leave.

Imogen   Oh, hello, Kenneth. I think you're *really* funny.

Sid   Well, that makes two of you.

Imogen   No, you make me laugh, you really do. You're my favourite. (*Pause.*) And you are too. You're both my favourites. You really make me laugh. I only have to look at you. Both.

Kenneth   Your immaculate taste is matched solely by your critical discernment.

Imogen   Thank you.

Sid   Make yourself at home.

Imogen   Thank you. Ooh. It's a very amusing script, isn't it?

Kenneth   I'd say its overt humour resonates in inverse proportion to its inherent dramatic qualities, yes.

Sid   You're right; it's a clever script.

Imogen   Saluté.

Sid *laughs with her.* **Kenneth** *silent.*

Imogen   Infamy, infamy . . .

She laughs again, **Kenneth** *sneers approval.* **Sid** *silent.*

Kenneth   Yes. He nicked it, of course. Gets all his best gags from old radio scripts. Denis Norden should sue.

Sid   I'll catch you later then.

Kenneth   If you think I'm being fobbed off just so you can get your end away, you've another thing coming.

Imogen   Get your what away?

Sid   Take no notice. (*To* **Kenneth**.) Shove off.

Kenneth   I want to know how you got ensconced in a Merry Traveller.

Sid   Don't mind us. Professional banter.

Kenneth   Quite frankly, this favouritism is a fucking disgrace.

Sid   Would you like a little something to ward off the chill?

Imogen   Oh, no thank you. I don't drink.

Sid   Dontcha? That's . . . me neither.

Imogen   Bit of a health freak, I'm afraid.

Sid   Very wise.

Imogen   Vegetarian too.

Sid   That's amazing; so am I.

Imogen   Really? What a coincidence. What sign are you?

Kenneth   A406 Chiswick Roundabout.

Sid   Shuddup. What sign are *you*?

Imogen   I'm Libra.

Sid   I don't believe it.

Kenneth   Neither do I.

Sid   It's not often you meet a fellow librarian.

Imogen   I'd really like to get all this off.

Sid   Likewise, I'm sure. We'll give you a bit of privacy here; *voilà*.

He cantilevers the wardrobe doors to partition the interior.

Imogen   Oh, that's very clever, isn't it?

Sid   Shower's through here. On and off. Hot and cold.

Imogen   Fabulous. This is really sweet of you.

Sid   Can't have you going home like that.

Imogen   See you in a while, then.

Sid   Take your time, sweetheart.

She shutters herself into the ablution compartment.

Kenneth   Vegetarian?

Sid   I've eaten vegetables.

Kenneth   Lambs to the slaughter with you, isn't it?

Sid   You've got a mouth like a sewer and I couldn't care less, but when there's a lady in the room you keep your filthy gob shut, all right?

Kenneth   Are you even slightly conscious that your urge to protect that poor girl's honour is somewhat at odds with your shameless desire to shag her?

Sid   Lovely backside.

Kenneth   I thought not.

Sid *looks at his watch.*

Sid   Strewth. I'm missing the four o'clock.

Turns on a portable TV.

It amazes me, a bloke like you. How you can't appreciate a bird like that is beyond me.

Kenneth   Spare me the pity. Those sporadic pleasures of the flesh I do enjoy I have no intention of sharing with anyone else.

Imogen *cries out orgasmically, off.*

Sid   What's up?

Imogen   It's cold.

Sid   Turn the dooh-dah.

Imogen   I have turned the dooh-dah.

Sid   You have to turn the electric on; I'll show you.

Imogen   No, wait!

Sid   Close your eyes and I'll come in.

Kenneth   Under starter's orders.

Imogen *in bathtowel, pops her head round.*

Imogen   You have to what?

Kenneth   And they're off.

Sid   Little switch just there. Little red light. It has to heat up. Come and have a drink while you're waiting.

Imogen   No, that's all right; I've got to . . . um and er – all sorts of things. I'm going to the premiere of *Dr Zhivago* tonight.

Sid   That's nice, who with?

Imogen   Oh, I never know 'til I get in the limo. Lovely.

She shutters herself in.

Kenneth   Not exactly your intellectual equal, is she? Which about puts her on par with a jellyfish.

Sid   Number six. On the rails.

Kenneth   It's not the money. I'd be mortified to take a penny more for peddling this sort of tosh.

Sid   Come on, you stupid sodding mare.

Kenneth   It's the tacit acknowledgment of one's contribution . . .

Sid   Don't go round, go through, go . . . Oh, Jesus.

Kenneth   A bit of appreciation, that's all I'm asking. A bit of gratitude.

Sid   You hopeless bloody mare. That's not a racehorse, that's three hundredweight of bleeding catfood, that is.

Punches the TV and turns it off.

Kenneth   Spending any time whatsoever in your company leaves one with a giddying sense of *déjà vu*.

Sid   Can you lend us a pony?

Kenneth   You see what I mean?

Sid   Please?

Kenneth   You already owe me fifty.

Sid   Well, you're daft enough, then.

Kenneth   If you ever won, I'd understand it.

Sid   If every bird you tried to shag said yes, there'd be no point chasing 'em, would there?

Kenneth   If every bird *you* tried to shag said yes, you wouldn't be able to chase them; you'd be in a rest home.

Sid   I can't help it; I love those little gee-gees. Go on; lend us a hundred and fifty.

Kenneth   No.

Sid   I thought we were mates.

Kenneth   I'm nobody's mate, thank you.

Sid   We go back a long way, you and I.

Kenneth   That's as maybe, but we've nothing in common.

Sid   Nonsense.

Kenneth   Name me one thing.

Sid   Well . . .

Kenneth   You see.

Sid   Hawtrey. We've both been goosed by Hawtrey.

Kenneth   Yes, but you punched him.

Sid   He's thrown up on both of us.

Kenneth   That's your definition of 'mates', is it? Fifteen years verbal abuse, then five minutes rinsing chow mein off each other's trousers? Hardly the Musketeers, is it?

Sid   We never fancied Hawtrey, *but* . . .

Both   . . . we both got screwed by Hancock.

Kenneth   True.

Sid   Bastard.

Kenneth   All for one and every man for himself.

Sid   I only need a monkey.

Kenneth   No.

Sid   No wonder he dropped you.

Kenneth   He dropped you too.

Sid   He dropped you before he dropped me.

Kenneth   But he told me to my face.

Sid   I passed him the other day. I was driving down Piccadilly. He crossed the street ahead of me. Looked as if he hadn't slept for a week. Unshaven . . . he looked dreadful, quite dreadful. So full of liquor he didn't see me. I got the car parked but he'd gone.

Kenneth   Serves him right.

Sid   Have you no compassion?

Kenneth   Yes, and I'm saving it all for myself.

Barbara (*off*)   Hello-oh? Anybody home?

Sid   Gawd blimey.

Barbara   Kenneth?

Kenneth   Who is it?

Sid   It's her. Double-O whatsit.

Enter **Barbara**. *Short, blonde, buxom. Outrageous wardrobe accentuating her wiggle. Twenty-five years old.*

Barbara   It's only me.

Kenneth   Oh, hello.

Barbara   Just popped in to say hello. Am I interrupting?

Kenneth   I can't imagine what.

Barbara   Give us a snog, then.

Kenneth   Off camera? I should cocoa.

Barbara   Mmmmwha!

Kenneth   Charmed, I'm sure.

Barbara   Hello. You're Sidney.

Sid   Yes.

Barbara   I'm Barbara.

Sid   Yes.

Pause. **Sid** *is besotted.*

Barbara   It's really nice to meet you.

Sid   Yes.

Barbara   Thirty-six C.

Sid   What?

Barbara   You'll get used to them. Have a good butcher's. I don't mind a good ogle, it's all those surreptitious glances drive me mad. I get double vision just trying to establish eye contact.

Sid   Right.

Barbara   Am I stopping you getting undressed?

Kenneth   Chance'd be a fine thing.

Barbara   He's got good knees, hasn't he?

Kenneth   I don't wish to venture an opinion.

Barbara   You've got good knees.

Sid   Thank you.

Barbara   You can tell a lot about a man from his knees. Only good reason for getting his trousers off.

Kenneth   Good God in heaven, he's blushing.

Sid   Shut your face. Would you like a drink?

Barbara   That'd be nice.

Sid   Have a sit down.

Barbara   I can't stay long. I only popped in to give Kenny an invite.

Kenneth   You should paint the walls that colour.

Barbara   Leave him alone.

Kenneth   I hadn't expected to see you here. I heard they offered you Second Slave Girl and you told them to shove it.

Barbara   I did n'all. Only three lines and two of them were feeds. No, they're doing some re-recording on *Spying*. I had to pop in to dub me 'buttocks'.

Kenneth   I told 'em they'd have to dub your 'buttocks'.

Barbara   I had to say 'bottom' instead. You'd think that would lip-synch, wouldn't you, but it was a real sodding effort.

Kenneth   Buttocks.

Barbara   Bottom.

Kenneth *mouths 'Buttocks' as* **Barbara** *says:*

Barbara   Bottom.

Kenneth *mouths 'Bottom' as* **Barbara** *says:*

Barbara   Buttocks.

Barbara   Bollocks. That'd fit. But 'bottom', honestly.

Kenneth   I told Gerald he wouldn't get his 'buttocks' passed, in or out of context. But he rattled on about comic integrity. I told him, it doesn't matter how funny buttocks are, if Rothwell insists on rubbing our noses in 'em every five minutes the Lord Chamberlain is fully justified in his opinion of us as purveyors of utter filth.

Sid   Here we go.

Kenneth   Yes, well, I'm sick to death of serving the fantasies of that inefficient hack! For all our expertise we're producing culture far cruder than the bloody Tudors. Our entertainments echo our dilemmas. Permanent values are being utterly neglected, and the devouring grasp of the cheap gag has strangled the spirit.

Barbara   Oh, don't bang on, Kenny. Have an invite. It's not a big do or anything; it's just nip in the registry and pop down the boozer afterwards.

Sid   Can I come?

Barbara   Er . . . yes, if you like. You can come to the pub.

Sid   I love a wedding.

Barbara   It's not really a wedding. Haven't got time for all that palaver. It's just a way of saying, you know; me and him.

Sid   No honeymoon then?

Barbara   Sod off; he's not getting away with no honeymoon. Can't decide where to go though.

Kenneth   Madeira's nice, apparently.

Barbara   Where the cake comes from?

Kenneth   It's where Kenneth Horne goes. Round the Horne to Maderia.

Barbara   Can you drink the water?

Kenneth   I don't know. I don't do foreign. I did foreign in the war; I shall never do foreign again.

Barbara   That's why you're so pasty.

Kenneth   I'll have you know men of this complexion built the Empire.

Barbara   You could do with a bit of sun.

Kenneth   On this pittance?

Barbara   Ronnie deserves a nice holiday after Wandsworth nick.

Kenneth   How's he settling?

Barbara   Oh, not bad. I met him at the gates, you know. We got a taxi back to the flat. I'd had the whole place newly redecorated.

Kenneth   Did he like it?

Barbara   Well, he liked the bedroom ceiling.

Sid   What was he in for?

Barbara   He was fitted up. Receiving. I ask you. Ronnie; receiving. Doping greyhounds is about his mark. I daren't use anything out of the bathroom cabinet, and I've got a fridge full of mince.

Sid   I've just realised who we're talking about. He knocks about with the Krays, doesn't he?

Barbara   No, he doesn't. I do.

Sid   Oh.

Barbara   And they're not up for discussion, all right?

Sid   Fair enough.

Barbara   Co-ercion my arse. The only bit of coercion I know about was the premiere of *Sparrows* when they coerced five hundred people to cheer me all down the Old Kent Road, so I'm having no one knocking 'em, all right?

Sid   I wasn't knocking 'em.

Barbara   Good.

Sid   You can tell 'em I wasn't.

Barbara   Right.

Sid   Don't tell 'em I was 'cos I wasn't.

Barbara   All right.

Sid   Don't mention me at all, in fact.

Barbara   Oh, give over. Are you married, Sid?

Sid   Married alive.

Barbara   Long time?

Sid   Seventeen years.

Barbara   Ahh.

Sid   And a few before that.

Barbara   Years?

Sid   Wives. Take my advice; don't get married. Just find someone you don't like and buy them a house.

Barbara (*laughs*)   No, don't. Ronnie's been married before. He was married when I met him. I was with him nine months before I found out; he was working us in shifts.

Sid   This is the man you're going to marry?

Barbara   I went berserk. Have you ever been unfaithful, Sidney?

Sid   Naah.

Sound of running water off, and a sensual sigh from **Imogen**.

Kenneth   And her backside's more impressive than her timing.

Barbara   You cheeky devil; you've got a girl in there.

Sid   I'm doing her a favour.

Barbara   Is that what your wife would think?

Sid   My wife trusts me. You trust yours?

Barbara   He won't mess around again.

Sid   A leopard cannot change its spots.

Barbara   No, but it can have its balls cut off.

Phone rings, **Sid** *answers it.*

Sid (*phone*) Hello? Yes, I'll tell him. Your presence is required in the Holy Temple of the Vestal Virgins. And a lot of good it'll do 'em.

Kenneth Oh, it's all utter pap.

Sid What about that two bob?

Kenneth I haven't got two bob.

Sid Come on, mate, I'm in deep manure.

Kenneth Don't mate me.

Sid Val's going to kill me.

Kenneth I shouldn't worry; she's bound to be acquitted. Come on. I wouldn't advise you to plant your derrière here; you're not safe.

Sid She's safe as houses in here.

Kenneth Safe as houses in Dresden. If you stay here he'll have his hand in your purse in thirty seconds, and that'll be the hand nearest daylight.

Sid Have another drink. Put your feet up.

Kenneth Up where he likes 'em, keeping his ears warm.

Sid Will you shut it!

Barbara Oh, don't argue. I've got to go anyway. It was very nice to meet you.

Sid *Enchanté*, I'm sure. Come again, any time.

Barbara Thank you. You're a sweetheart.

She pecks him on the cheek.

Barbara Bye, then.

Sid Bye.

Kenneth *and* **Barbara** *leave the van and cross the lot.* **Sid** *gazes after them, prancing from one window to the next. Still hidden,* **Imogen** *starts to sing 'For All We Know'.*

Kenneth   Evening, ladies.

Kenneth *lifts his skirt. Some girls out of view scream and giggle.*

Barbara   Oh, put it away, please.

Kenneth   Beauty is in the eye of the beholder, so one feels beholden to give 'em an eyeful.

Kenneth *laughs his machine-gun laugh, and they disappear.* **Sid** *listens until the phone rings.*

Sid (*phone*)   Yeh? Hello, Bernie. Well ... why not? No, no, mate; she's new; she's got the wrong end of the stick. She's going to Freddie to pick up some winnings. I need a bit from you 'cause I want to get a little present for Val. Bernie, would I lie to you? All right, but listen, mate; it's a dead cert and when it comes in I'm gonna get Val something really special. What do you mean, a divorce? Bernie ... !

He puts the phone down and drinks. He seems pressured. **Imogen** *finishes singing and emerges.*

Imogen   Hello.

Sid   Hello.

Imogen   Everyone gone?

Sid   Yep.

Imogen   You've got lipstick.

Sid   Whoops.

He wipes off **Barbara**'s *lipstick.*

Imogen   She's nice. She gave me a lovely smile earlier.

Sid   Yeh. She's got a nice smile.

He folds the tissue carefully and puts it in his pocket.

Imogen   She's very friendly for a short person. She's not a real blonde though. Although that's quite a good thing, because real blondes are usually much stupider than artificial ones; had you noticed that?

Sid I had as a matter of fact.

Imogen And far less aggressive in my experience. You like her, don't you?

Sid ... I'm very affable.

Imogen Is that your type? Short blondes?

Sid Absolutely. Unless there's an r in the month.

Imogen It's May.

Sid Or a y. That was a very nice song you were singing.

Imogen My father used to sing it.

Sid You get on well with your father?

Imogen Daddy's dead. He died.

Sid Oh, I'm sorry. Did you love him?

Imogen Um ... well, yes. I loved him very much.

Sid That's nice. Do you like fruit?

Imogen Yes.

Sid Want some?

Imogen Um ...

Sid Have some.

He offers her a different exotic fruit.

Imogen Thank you.

Sid That's a passion fruit.

Imogen Is it?

Sid That's right.

Imogen Why?

Sid I've no idea. Try it.

Imogen I've never had a passion fruit.

Sid Well, you can't just bite into it because the skin is very bitter. The flesh on the other hand is very sweet. So before you can eat you have to pull back the skin like so, and there's the flesh, look.

Imogen Wow.

Sid Those taste buds tingling?

Imogen It's beautiful inside.

Sid Isn't it? In you go.

Imogen Mmm. Wow.

Sid Use your tongue.

Imogen I am.

Sid How's that?

Imogen It's . . .

Sid Mmm?

Imogen Delicious. Mmph; I'm all wet.

Sid Stay that way; it gets better. Move over.

Imogen Do you want some?

Sid No, you enjoy yourself.

Imogen Here.

Sid You temptress. Cor.

Imogen Good?

Sid That's good, isn't it?

Imogen That's very good.

Sid Here; let me.

Imogen No, no; you.

Sid No no, after you.

They feed each other. He wipes the corner of her mouth with his finger and tastes her.

Imogen   Ooh. I'm all sticky.

Sid   You taste good.

Imogen   Have you got a tissue?

Sid   Who needs tissues? Here.

He turns her head towards him and leans towards her. **Barbara** *enters.*

Barbara   Are you decent? I suddenly remembered I'd forgotten something.

Sid   What was that then?

Barbara   I can't remember. Oh, hello.

Imogen   Hello.

Barbara   Are you Imogen?

Imogen   Yes, hello.

Barbara   There's a driver looking for you.

Imogen   Oh, heavens. I'm late. All sticky.

Barbara   Whoops.

Imogen   Thanks for the shower and the thingy.

Sid   Any time.

Imogen   Bye, then.

Barbara   Bye, love.

Imogen   Bye, Sid.

Sid   Bye bye.

Imogen   Byyye.

Exit **Imogen**.

Barbara   Now. Keys.

She finds them in her hand.

Barbara   Oh, here they are. Silly me.

Sid   You're jumping to conclusions.

Barbara   You're old enough to be her father.

Sid   Precisely; I was taking a paternal interest.

Barbara   You were taking a liberty. Poor girl's got enough stars in her eyes; she doesn't need one in her knickers.

Sid   Does your husband-to-be mind?

Barbara   Mind what?

Sid   You practising on other men.

Barbara   Cheeky sod.

Sid   Mind your language.

Barbara   Mind your own bloody business.

Sid   I can't abide a woman cursing.

Barbara   I can't abide a womaniser.

Sid   It's come to something when a bloke can't have an intelligent chat with a girl . . .

Barbara   A girl can't have an intelligent chat with two tongues in her mouth!

Sid   This is tragic. A lovely woman like you. Put a ring on your finger, suddenly you're every man's missus.

Barbara   One man's missus.

Sid   God help him.

Barbara   I'll drink to that.

Sid   I've got whisky, vodka, gin . . .

He opens a wardrobe to reveal an extraordinary selection.

Barbara   Fucking hell.

Sid (*winces*)   Oy.

Barbara   I mean; my, my, what a marvellous selection

of beverages.

Sid How about a Martini?

Barbara Does anyone get out of here vertical?

Sid You've got the wrong idea about me.

Barbara That's me and the entire British Isles then.

Sid No no no; you're mistaking the man for the screen persona! I may come across as lewd and licentious, but in actual fact I'm very respectful of the opposite sex.

Barbara Pull the other one.

Sid I was trying to.

Barbara I know you were!

Sid I ask you; is this the face of a reprobate? Secret of a good Martini is to make it relatively dry. Good measure of gin, nice little olive, then make sure it's had a good look at the other bottle. Cheers.

Barbara Oh, all right. Just the one. I do know what you mean; people take one look at me and make all sorts of presumptions.

Sid All of 'em insulting, all of 'em wrong. It's a disgrace.

Barbara You're right. I'm sorry.

Sid God help him.

Barbara God help him. He'll need it. When he went inside I wasn't as well known as I am now, and he finds that hard. We've tried going back to the old places, but there's always someone with a grudge along the bar. One bloke asked me to sign a ten-bob note then blew his nose on it. That was the end of his nose. Be warned. Ronnie's sense of justice is always strictly anatomical.

Sid I've told you; if you're fixed up I respect that. If you're getting married I'm not interested. Would you like some fruit?

Barbara   No, I'm fine.

Sid   Have a piece of fruit; it's good for you.

Barbara   I'm not really bothered.

Sid   I'm not talking Coxes here; I'm talking serious fruit.

Barbara   What sort of fruit?

Sid   Ever tried one of these?

He offers her yet another type of exotic fruit.

Barbara   What is it?

Sid   Passion fruit.

Barbara   Where's it come from?

Sid   Tahiti.

Barbara   I don't think I'd like it.

Sid   Well, you won't know that 'til you've tried it, will you?

Barbara   Oh, go on then.

Sid   You can't just bite into it because the skin is very bitter. The flesh on the other hand is very sweet. So before you can eat you have to pull back the skin like so, and there's the flesh, look.

Barbara   Oh, it's all pink.

Sid   If it could talk it'd be saying eat me.

Barbara   Give me the knife.

Sid   No, no.

Barbara   I want to cut a bit off.

Sid   You can't do that. That'd be sacrilege. Watch. Do as I do. Like this. Then like this.

Barbara   Oh, I see; like cunnilingus.

He chokes. She gets up, passing the fruit bowl.

And when you've finished that ... have a banana.

And leaves him holding one.

Blackout.

Act Two

Scene One

Camping. 1969.

The caravan is a little the worse for wear; cluttered with years of use. It now stands in the middle of a field near Ruislip. It's raining heavily. **Kenneth** *and* **Sid** *sit miserably in front of a single-bar fire.*

Kenneth We're never going to get out of this field.

Sid Count your blessings.

Kenneth We're going to sink without trace.

Sid Go sit on the bus, then.

Kenneth No longer welcome. I irritate the lesser mortals.

Sid You irritate me and all. Get back to the bus.

Kenneth I would if you didn't owe me three hundred quid.

Sid If I didn't owe you three hundred quid you'd have to, mate. You wouldn't be here in the first place. If everyone I owed money to took this sort of advantage, we *would* bloody sink.

Kenneth They're fools to themselves.

Sid And don't disparage my generosity; it cost me a fiver to get Horace to run a cable from the genny.

Kenneth My fiver.

Sid Not your fiver.

Kenneth Someone's fiver.

Sid Your fiver's long gone, mate. You couldn't lend us five hundred, could you?

Kenneth   Five hundred?!

Sid   I've had a bit of a dodgy run.

Kenneth   That's half your entire fee

Sid   There's a dead cert at Newbury.

Kenneth   You had a dead cert at Aintree last week. It fell at the third and they shot it. Don't come much deader than that.

Sid   Come on, mate, I'm desperate.

Kenneth   It's the lavatory gets up my nose.

Sid   Here we go again.

Kenneth   You'd think with my arse I'd be the one to get given me own lavatory.

Sid   You're not the only one with an arse.

Kenneth   Bitter bloody misery it is, my fundament.

Sid   How big are they, these legendary haemorrhoids of yours?

Kenneth   I can't imagine what possible concern that's ever going to be of yours.

Sid   Me neither, mate.

Kenneth   I shall survive without your concern and can certainly do without your curiosity.

Sid   Then stop banging on about them.

Kenneth   Bum trouble's just a dirty joke to the likes of you, because you've never suffered. You wouldn't know and haven't the wit to imagine the abject creeping horror of an ailing anus.

Sid   Will you give it a rest!

Kenneth   The agony of it, the endless suffering, the wretched torment . . .

Sid   You don't know what suffering is, mate; I've had

piles the size of tomatoes for twenty bloody years.

Kenneth   First I've heard of it.

Sid   That's because I don't dish 'em up every bloody mealtime. Unlike you I don't feel the urge to bring every conversation round to my backside. I've got piles'd put yours right in the shade, mate.

Kenneth   You are quite unbelievably competitive.

Sid   Five hundred quid.

Kenneth   What?

Sid   Five hundred quid I've got twice as many as you, and half as many to the pound.

Kenneth   This is all part of your pitifully desperate desire to prove yourself somehow superior to myself. So demonstrably hopeless a quest it was inevitable it would come down to arseholes eventually.

Sid   You want a butcher's?

Kenneth   I most certainly do not.

Sid   Then let's change the bleeding subject.

Kenneth   Didn't have you down for bum trouble. Who are you under?

Sid   How's that?

Kenneth   Which consultant; Berry or Hadfield?

Sid   Me GP.

Kenneth   Your GP? You can't trust some GP off Gunnersbury Avenue with your anus. You want your bum in the hands of a Harley Street man. You need Dr Berry. Berry's the man you need. I've gone off Hadfield.

Sid   Why?

Kenneth   One tends to go off bum doctors very suddenly. For reasons it's scarcely necessary to go into. How bad are they?

Sid Torture.

Kenneth Eleven in the morning?

Sid Living hell. And purgatory about . . .

Both . . . four o'clock.

Kenneth I know.

Sid Why is that?

Kenneth The bowel moves in mysterious but predictable ways. You shouldn't do breakfast.

Sid I can't not do breakfast.

Kenneth And curry! God in his heaven, you eat curry.

Sid I can't not eat curry.

Kenneth I daren't even glance at a dhansak. A chilli con carne, possibly, at lunchtime, with plenty of yoghurt.

Sid Yoghurt? I'd rather be dead.

Kenneth Eat another vindaloo and you might be.

Sid I've had some worrying mornings, admittedly. I have to admit it can get a bit lonely.

Kenneth You had the elastic bands?

Sid I don't want to talk about it.

Kenneth The deep icy probing . . . the sharp prick of that horrible hypodermic.

Sid Yes, thank you. That's enough.

Kenneth The twang of rubber as it grips the doomed fillip of your mutating organ . . .

Sid Will you shut your face!

Kenneth Then he says keep an eye out for them! I should cocoa. I've not looked down a toilet for forty years and I don't intend to start now.

Sid Please, let's change the subject. Do you want a gin?

Kenneth   Don't mind if I do. Have you got a bitter lemon?

Sid   No, I just had a shower.

They laugh.

Sid   To suffering.

Kenneth   Yes.

Sid   In silence.

Kenneth   I'd always believed you and I had nothing in common. One of the touchstones of my very existence has crumbled to dust. All the Greeks had 'em you know. All the great philosophers.

Sid   That's because they spent too much time with their heads up their arses.

Kenneth   Hancock had 'em.

Sid   You don't kill yourself because your backside hurts.

Kenneth   Well, it would be pretty ridiculous.

Sid   I wish I'd caught up with him, that day in Piccadilly.

Kenneth   Wouldn't have made a blind bit of difference.

Sid   Don't you believe it; things like that, chance encounters, change people's lives.

Kenneth   But to do it in Australia. Why Australia?

Sid   You ever been?

Kenneth   No.

Sid   Makes perfect sense. See Venice and die, see Melbourne and top yourself.

Kenneth   The man was mediocre. He slammed the door on everyone responsible for his success, and when he realised what he'd done, he slammed it on himself.

Sid   You know what you are; you're a misanthrope, that's what you are.

Kenneth   Define misanthrope.

Sid   You.

Kenneth   But what's it mean?

Sid   I don't know.

Kenneth   I didn't think you did.

Sid   Bernie said you're a misanthrope and Bernie's a scholar.

Kenneth   Well, he's right. I've never met anyone who wasn't running around trying to make sense of their lives by inflicting their sexual organs on everyone else. Or mewling in despair at the realisation they're nothing more than a rotting bag of bones.

Sid   I'll put you out in the rain again.

A knock on the door.

Barbara   Kenneth, are you in there?

Sid   He's always in here.

Barbara *enters in mac and bikini with green feet.*

Barbara   They've had to stop; they found a fish in the gate. Look at my feet.

Sid   Impossible.

Barbara   There wasn't any grass in the field, so they've sprayed the mud green. There's four props boys in sou'westers up an elm tree sticking leaves on. One of them fell out; he looks like the Jolly Green Giant. I'm dying for a wee.

Sid   I wouldn't go in there if I were you.

Barbara   Why not?

Kenneth   Sidney's left possibly his greatest performance in it.

Barbara   Oh, charming.

Sid   Well, for God's sake; it's my toilet.

Barbara   You could have flushed it.

Sid   The little flap's stuck.

Barbara   Do you think it's like this at Universal Studios?

Kenneth   I'm still damp from this morning.

Sid   You wouldn't be damp if you'd stop messing about and got on with it.

Kenneth   I was enjoying myself.

Sid   Acting's not something you enjoy. It's something you do and go home.

Barbara   What's got up your nose?

Kenneth   I corpsed him.

Sid   You did not corpse me!

Kenneth   You grinned.

Sid   I did not grin, I grimaced.

Kenneth   He had a bet on with the clapper-loader he wouldn't go to a second take all week.

Sid   I don't need a second take.

Barbara   Unless it's snogging.

Sid   And you call yourself a professional!

Kenneth   I certainly do.

Sid   A professional does not mug on his reverses.

Barbara   He always mugs on his reverses. Sends me right up.

Sid   It's undisciplined.

Barbara   It's funny.

Sid   Which is more than I can say for his close-ups.

Kenneth There's nothing wrong with my close-ups. There's a laugh in every one of them; I make sure of it.

Sid I've noticed. Never mind the sense of the scene.

Kenneth Oh bugger the sense; it's the delivery they laugh at.

Sid I'm an actor, mate.

Kenneth You're a cheap vaudevillian, whereas I'm a classically trained thesbian. I have worked with Orson Welles.

Sid So have I.

Kenneth I have played Shakespeare.

Sid Well, so have I.

Kenneth I have read a book.

Sid *sniffs.* **Kenneth** *wins.*

Kenneth I have sat on the steps of the Coliseum and debated the nature of man with Sophocles, I have.

Kenneth *farts.*

Barbara Kenny.

Sid Bloody hell.

Barabara Honestly. How you expect to maintain a decent working relationship with people I have no idea.

Kenneth Rudolph Valentino was a farter. His leading ladies never complained.

Barbara They were silent films.

Kenneth I consider it one of my more singular accomplishments that I can display an uncommon degree of eloquence . . . (*Another little fart.*) . . . from both ends simultaneously.

Barbara Oh, take it outside, for heaven's sake!

Sid   And don't come back.

Kenneth   I'm not leaving you two alone.

Barbara   Why not?

Kenneth   You ought to watch it. In and out of here all the time. People are beginning to talk.

Sid   What people?

Barbara   Who?

Kenneth   The entire unit, that's who.

Barbara   Well, not that it's any of their business, but I happen to be a happily married woman, all right?

Kenneth   That why you blubbed all the way to the registry, muttering you'd rather be shot?

Barbara   I might have had a decent marriage if I hadn't had a lousy honeymoon.

Kenneth   Wasn't my fault you had a lousy honeymoon.

Barbara   How do you know I had a lousy honeymoon?

Kenneth   I was there.

Barbara   Precisely. If you hadn't been there, Kenny, perhaps it wouldn't have been so lousy. Perhaps if your mother hadn't been there I might have had a few hours alone with my husband. Perhaps if you and your mother and your sister hadn't been there, there might have been a moment's silence during which we might have heard a parrot or something.

Kenneth   You had a lousy honeymoon because you booked us all on a cheap package flight which dumped us next to nowhere so we had to get a packet boat from hell to Funchal in a force eight gale from which I for one have never recovered!

Barbara   You shouldn't have eaten your dinner with the boat at forty-five degrees.

Kenneth   I paid for it, I'll bloody well eat it.

Barbara   There were fifty-year-old sailors threw up just watching you.

Kenneth   And it rained all bloody week. I wish I'd never invited meself.

Barbara   I thought you might distract us from the slow realisation we'd actually done it.

Kenneth   It smells in here. It smells of rot. I'm going to see if the caterers are still afloat.

Kenneth *leaves.*

Barbara   Christ, I'm cold. Give us a Scotch.

Sid   I dreamed about you last night.

Barbara   Did you?

Sid   No, you wouldn't let me. Whenever you walk in the room . . .

Barbara   Don't start.

Sid   I can't help it.

Barbara   I can't handle it.

Sid   I know I'm old, I'm out of condition, I've never been a looker . . .

Barbara   Stop it.

Sid   Self-pity, I know, that's not attractive in a man.

Barbara   Do you have to jump in the deep end every time there's only two of us. Couldn't we talk about the weather or something?

Sid   It's raining. I love you.

Barbara   No you don't. You fancy me and I'm having none of it and that's the end of the matter.

Sid   I love you.

Barbara   Sidney, how old are you?

Sid   Fifty-two.

Barbara   Fifty-six. How old am I?

Sid   Seventeen.

Barbara   I'm thirty-two. Now what's that about, Sidney? Why can't you fancy someone your own age?

Sid   Have you seen the women my age? Have you kissed one? Their lips go all furry. The back of their thighs go all puddeny.

Barbara   Sidney.

Sid   I like 'em young. It's a sexual whatsname, innit? Preference. You don't go around telling Ken and Charlie to find a good woman, do you? But you treat me like a dirty old sod.

Barbara   You are a dirty old sod.

Sid   Is that why you don't fancy me?

Barbara   Sid, I don't *not* fancy you . . .

Sid   You don't not?

Barbara   I love you to bits; you know that.

Sid   So you do fancy me?

Barbara   I didn't say that, I said I didn't not.

Sid   Well, you do or you don't.

Barbara   No, Sid, I will or I won't and I'm not going to.

Sid   You said if I stopped fooling around you'd think about it.

Barbara   I did not. I said you'd be more attractive and you would.

Sid   I haven't looked at another woman for months.

Barbara   Sid, you're married. So am I. And Ronnie's got a sniff of this, you know.

Sid Has he?

Barbara He's given me a driver.

Sid That big bloke?

Barbara Yeh, so watch it.

Sid Thing is ...

Barbara Sid, will you please change the subject!

Sid It's still raining. I still love you.

Barbara It'd be the end of our friendship.

Sid All your objections are clichés.

Barbara This whole thing's a cliché.

Sid First time I clapped eyes on you ...

Barbara You had a woman in your shower.

Sid (*suddenly shouts*) I'm not interested in anyone else! Why do you insist on treating me like this ...

He grabs a script and yanks it open.

... arsehole, this lecherous leering fucking ... bastard!!

He tears up the script with surprising violence. **Barbara** *shocked to silence.*

I don't want anyone else. It's you I want.

Barbara (*genuinely sorry*) Oh, Sidney.

She touches him and he takes immediate advantage, embracing her. Suddenly they're kissing; a mutual passion. She pulls away.

Barbara You're a good kisser, I'll give you that.

Sid I'm good all over.

Barbara Are you? I bet you are.

Lights fade.

Scene Two

Camping (continued).

Later in the day. The partitions are closed. No one's to be seen, but the caravan is rocking gently with an unmistakably rhythmic rattle and squeak. **Sally** *appears in a hurry, staggering through the mud in huge wellingtons, carrying a suit and a selection of trilbys. She stops when she recognises the motion. Turns back, looks at her watch, dithers, then shouts.*

Sally   Sid!

Various noises off announce a sudden uncoupling and a bruised shin.

Sid (*off*)   Gawd, strewth.

Imogen   Sssh!

Sid *stumbles into the main part of the van as* **Sally** *goes round the outside and enters.*

Sally   They've rescheduled, Sid; they want you in ten minutes.

Sid   Gawd blimey.

Sally   Nice lunch?

Sid   I was just learning me lines.

Sally   You've only got one line and you know it off by heart. So do the rest of us.

Sid   For one terrible moment I thought you were her.

Sally   Serve you right if it had been.

Sid   Sally; the thing I admire most in a woman is discretion.

Sally   No, Sid; the thing you admire most in a woman is yourself. This is for Barbara.

Sid   What is it?

Sally   Fishing-line. These trousers, that jacket. Hat's not continuity so choose one, I've got to see to Bernie. I'll be back in five minutes. Be ready, all right.

Sid   Sally; mum's the word.

Sally   No, Sid; wanker's the word.

Sally *leaves.* **Sid** *goes to the partition.*

Sid   All right; she's gone. You'd better get a move on before anyone else barges in.

Imogen *enters from behind the partition. She's drunk and not as vivacious as when we first met her. She finds her scattered clothes.*

Imogen   I'm sorry.

Sid   What for?

Imogen   Causing an argument. I'm always causing arguments. If there's a man and there's me and then someone else there's usually an argument.

Sid   Take no notice. Sally's a bit repressed. She doesn't understand the liniments of healthy desire.

Imogen   I'm surprised you even remembered me. I'm flattered. I mean, who was I then? I was out and about, I know, but I'd barely left LAMDA and honestly I knew nothing. I *was* nothing. This is such a strange business. You get a job, you meet someone, you like them, you maybe sleep with them, the job ends, then you never see them again even though you always say you will. I made some really good friends on *When Dinosaurs Ruled the Earth*, except Raquel of course, but she doesn't make friends she just takes the odd hostage. Thing is I haven't seen anyone since. Except there was a particularly persistent caveman who I did see once but his wife was pregnant and he just cried all evening. Everything's so . . . temporary. That's what's nice about working with you lot; you're one big happy family. I'd love to work with you lot again.

Sid   I'm gonna be needed soon.

Imogen *carries on drinking.*

Imogen   Oh, that's all right; I only popped in to say

hello. You know what I wish? I wish I had smaller breasts.
Then I'd get to play some women with small breasts, and
they're always the best parts. I'd really like to play women
with no breasts at all, you know, like in Ibsen. I should
never have done the centrefold. I'm actually very versatile.
'An impressive multifaceted performance'; that's what they
said about me as Jenny Grubb in *Loving*. And that wasn't
just taking off the glasses and letting my hair down, that
was *acting* actually. I was *acting* her repressed sexuality. What
I'm saying is, I'm not just some stupid girl from Elmhurst
with a fucked knee, you know.

Sid   Right.

Imogen   I'm not just the Countess of Cleavage.

Sid   Absolutely.

Imogen   It's so hard to convince people I'm a serious
actress, but I really think it's beginning to happen. I've got
an audition for the Royal Shakespeare Company? And last
month I did *The Persuaders*. Only the pilot but both Roger
Moore *and* Tony Curtis were very complimentary and said
there was a very good chance my character could become
a regular.

Sid   I'm glad it's going well for you.

Imogen   Oh yes.

Sid   I'm glad you popped in.

Imogen   I'm glad too.

Sid   Thing is, um . . .

Imogen   Imogen.

Sid   Imogen. What we just did . . .

Imogen   I know, I know. I don't know why we did that I
mean I know you had a Royal Flush but I mean why so
suddenly I mean that's not why I came I don't want you to
think I'm a complete tart or anything I always liked you.

Sid   Well, these things happen.

Imogen   Yes they do; it's just a spontaneous thing and nothing to be ashamed of an expression of one's sexuality I hope you don't think I do this a lot.

Sid   I'm sure you don't.

Imogen   Because I don't. It's not why I came. I came because I wanted some advice.

Sid   What's that then?

Imogen   Well, you see, if I get the job with the Royal Shakespeare Company it's going to clash with *The Persuaders* if *The Persuaders* goes into a series, which it should, I mean it's got Roger Moore *and* Tony Curtis in it, but it's not definite and I'm not sure if I should do it. I'd rather be in the Royal Shakespeare Company but the problem is it's not a huge part, in fact I don't speak and I have to take my clothes off, but it *is* the RSC and Stratford's lovely. Anyway; you've done a bit of everything so I thought you might advise me. What do you think I should do?

Sid   *Persuaders*.

Imogen   But that's not definite.

Sid   Shakespeare then, definitely.

Imogen   But I haven't actually been offered it.

Sid   I'd take *The Persuaders*, then.

Imogen   But I don't want to act in rubbish, I want to act in really good stuff.

Sid   Then if I were you, I'd hang out for the Shakespeare.

Imogen   The money's not very good.

Sid   That's why I'd tend towards *The Persuaders*.

Imogen   Of course, I might not get offered either.

Sid   In which case, take the other one.

Imogen   I *need* a job. A proper job. I don't mean to

sound desperate but this not working; it's driving me mad.

Sid   I tell you what. I'll see what I can do.

Imogen   Oh, I didn't mean that you should . . .

Sid   No no no. No trouble.

Imogen   That's not what I . . . would you? I mean I hope you don't think that's why I came.

Sid   What are friends for?

Imogen   Hmmmm.

Sid   I'm going to have to get going.

Imogen   Daddy was on the board. Of LAMDA. I've never told anyone that. Anyway I mustn't be negative mustn't be negative mustn't be negative. Things can just turn right round, can't they? Round and round. Tonight even. I'm meeting Michael Winner for a drink at L'Escargot. Just for a chat, but you never know, do you?

Sid   That's right; you never know.

Imogen   I wouldn't mind doing a smallish part again if I was working with really good people.

Sid   I'll see what I can do.

Imogen   And what happened between us is a separate thing.

Sid   That's right.

Imogen   So if it happened again, well . . .

Sid   It mustn't happen again.

Imogen   Absolutely. That's what I . . . I mean if that's what you . . . that's fine.

Sid   You see, I'm being strictly monogamous at the moment.

Imogen   Oh, I'd hate to harm your marriage.

Sid   My marriage has nothing to do with it.

Imogen Oh. Well, this was . . . we both know what this was, this was . . .

Sid This was lovely.

Imogen I feel a bit woosy. I think I'd better lie down.

Sid You what?

Imogen Room's going round.

Sid Well, you'd better get some fresh air then.

Barbara *appears through the drizzle with* **Sally**, **Kenneth** *plodding on behind.* **Sid** *hears them approach.*

Barbara What's it doing in the van?

Sally I thought you were with Sid.

Barbara I'm not always with Sid.

Sid Second thoughts, perhaps you should have a little lie-down.

Imogen Thank you.

Barbara Why does everybody presume I'm with Sid.

Sally Well, you usually are sometimes.

Sid A nice quiet lie-down.

Imogen I think you're right.

Imogen *retires.*

Barbara Come on, Kenny; I want your honest opinion. I don't want to humiliate myself.

Kenneth You shouldn't have signed the contract then.

Imogen I usually come round in about half an hour.

Barbara Sidney.

Sid Who is it?

Barbara Only us. You don't mind if we do a bit of wardrobe in here do you?

Sid   Umm . . .

Barbara   It's not something I can do on the dining bus.

Sid   Well, what does he want?

Kenneth   Dry trousers, if you don't mind.

Sid   I do mind.

Kenneth   I don't care.

Sally   They're all under a tree, Sid; you've got another ten minutes.

Barbara *finds the fishing-line.*

Barbara   Bert still insists it's props. I said if it's sewn to my bra it's costume.

Sally   Give it here.

Barbara   If Bert does it it'll be thirteen takes.

Sally   I'll do it.

Sid   What you doing?

Barbara   Rehearsing. I just don't want to make a complete tit of myself.

Kenneth *laughs. She joins in.*

Barbara   No, stop it.

Sally *sews the line to* **Barbara**'*s bra.*

Sid   You should tell Gerald to stuff his nudity clause right up his nose.

Barbara   I know; Ronnie's going to do his nut.

Sid   If I was your husband I wouldn't let you do it.

Kenneth   But you're not, are you?

Sid   Don't start.

Kenneth   Well, I for one have always held the state of matrimony in the highest regard.

Sid   That is rich.

Kenneth   Together in the eyes of God.

Sid   What about your lot?

Kenneth   'Til death us do part.

Sid   Every last one of you . . .

Kenneth   Love, honour and obey.

Sid   Disgustingly promiscuous.

Kenneth   That's rich from a man who thinks Errol Flynn missed a lot of opportunities.

Sid   And he was bent, and all.

Kenneth   And almost as well-hung as me, apparently.

Sid   Only place you'd be well-hung is the Isle of Man.

Barbara   Sidney.

Sally   Done it.

Barbara   All right, unclip the dooh-dah, give it a good yank. Sid, turn your back.

Sid   Are you gonna tell the cameraman to turn his back?

Barbara   Turn round.

Sid   Point his arri in the opposite direction? (*He laughs.*)

Barbara   I want to practice getting me hands up.

Sid   I could help you there.

Barbara   Sidney.

Sid   Strewth.

Kenneth   Libidinous cretin.

Sid   You can talk. The moral climate's gone right down the pan since they legalised you lot.

Kenneth   Go on, that's right; assuage your own sordid

guilt by casting slurs on my entirely more refined sexual orientation.

Sid   I couldn't care less what you do to each other in private; it's your flouncing bleeding effeminacy gets up my nose.

Barbara   Sydney, turn round and face the wall.

Sid   It was bad enough, you and Charlie mincing through scene after scene; suddenly it's legal and you both turn into screaming queens.

Kenneth   I have never screamingly queened in my life.

Barbara   Ready?

Sally   Right.

Barbara   One, two . . . Sid; close the door.

Sid *closes the mirrored door.*

Barbara   One, two, three.

Sally *pulls the line.* **Barbara** *grabs her bra.* **Sid** *turns round.*

Sid   Ow!

Barbara   Serves you right. I knew you'd turn round.

Sid   I'm only flesh and blood.

Sally   You were too quick.

Barbara   You didn't pull hard enough.

Sally   I pulled really hard. Look, it's come off.

Sid   Here, let me.

Barbara   Get off. Go and find another horse to curse.

Sid   Gawd blimey, I'm missing the three o'clock.

Turns on his portable telly.

Kenneth   There's more to life than sex and horses, you know.

Sid   Shuttup, you poofta.

Barbara   Right, let's try again.

Kenneth   It's lucky you left South Africa. If the crops had failed you'd have shot your entire family.

Sid   Not before I'd shot you lot.

Barbara   Sidney! Watch your telly and no bloody peeping.

Kenneth   If you expect your average Odeon-full of punters to do the decent thing and all close their eyes in unison, I suggest you think again.

Barbara   God, I hate this.

Sid   Not to mention the crew.

Barbara   There won't be any crew; it'll be a closed set, don't you worry.

Sally   Turn round.

Sid   Blow me, they're almost home.

Sally   I'm going to use less tape.

Sid   Bloody thing.

He struggles with the aerial.

Barbara   I'm gonna keep me elbows bent so my hands are closer.

Sid   Where's Sudden Eclipse? Hold this, will you?

He gives **Sally** *the aerial.*

Sally   Yes sir, no sir, three bags full sir.

Barbara   Ready?

Sid   Hang on. They're neck and neck.

Sally   My tongue's free if anyone wants their shoes cleaning.

Sid   Come on, Sudden Eclipse.

Barbara   One . . .

Sid   Wait until they've crossed the line, will you?

Barbara Two . . .

Sid Hang on a minute . . .

Barbara Three.

Sally *pulls the line.* **Barbara**'s *bra flies off.* **Sid** *ricks his neck.*

Sid Ow!

Barbara Da da!

Kenneth Oh, Bravo!

Barbara What'd you see, Sid?

Sid Nothing. And I've ricked me bleedin' neck.

Barbara Serves you right. Give us me coat, Kenny.

Kenneth Ooh. Dresser on set.

Sally I've hurt me finger.

Sid Who's winning? Will you please get out of the way!

Sally Oh, pardon me for breathing.

Sally *falls out the caravan and disappears, tugging the aerial. The TV falls on* **Sid**'s *foot.*

Sid Ow!

Barbara What happened?

Sid Gawd Streuth!

Kenneth *and* **Barbara** *laugh.*

Sid What's so bloody funny?

Barbara Hard luck, Sid.

Sid I think I broke my toe.

Kenneth You're a voyeuristic disgrace and it serves you right.

Sid Unnatural acts, mate. Look in the Bible.

Kenneth That's right; throw your little stones. Hide

behind the ruined greenhouse of your own sad lechery. By all means pronounce judgement on the divine splinter of my sexual proclivities, if you can catch sight of it through the Epping Forest of your own lustful eye.

Sid Don't lecture me on sexual relationships, mate. Not from your perspective.

Barbara I wish you two'd pack it in.

Sid *returns the telly, that's still got some life in it.*

Sid Who won the bloody race?

Barbara You're really getting on my nerves.

Sid Lift up the aerial. Where's the bleedin' aerial? Sally, will you please ... Where's she gone?

Barbara Sally?

Sally *enters covered head to foot in mud, with a bent aerial.*

Sally Look at me! Look at the state of me!

Barbara Oh, Sally.

Sid Oh well, that's knackered, isn't it?

Barbara Lets get your clothes off.

Sid Good idea.

Barbara Leave her alone!

Kenneth It's incessant, isn't it? At least my lot are unfettered by the dual agendas of heterosexual desire.

Sid Oh, give it a rest.

Kenneth At least we're capable of frank and honest sexual relationships.

Sid Your lot? Relationships? What sort of relationship is it begins in a toilet and ends with a hammer in the head.

A stunned pause. **Kenneth** *goes to the door.*

Kenneth The boy shone. You met him. He made you

laugh. You liked him.

Kenneth *leaves*.

Barbara   Oh, Sidney.

Sid   Well.

Sally   I haven't got a change of clothes.

Barbara   Sidney, sort her out some clothes.

Sid   Who won the bloody race?

Sally   I don't care who won the bloody race. Whichever horse you didn't have money on won the bloody race!

Sid   If you'd held the aerial still it might have just nipped by on the inside.

Barbara   And the horrifying thing is: he believes that.

Sally   I bloody hate location.

Barbara   Calm down. Go take a shower.

Sid   No.

Barbara   Why not? Look at her.

Sid   All right then, but do it quietly.

Barbara   Why quietly?

Sid   I've got a splitting headache.

Sally   Good.

Sally *disappears*.

Sid   Do you fancy a drink?

Barbara   Vodka, please.

Sid   I meant let's go to a pub.

Barbara   I don't want us to be seen in a pub. I want to talk to you.

Sid   Let's go for a walk then.

Barbara   In this weather?

Sid   Bit of fresh air.

Barbara   Sidney, I want to talk.

Sid   We can talk in the dining bus.

Barbara   I want to talk about us.

Sid   Us?

Barbara   You snogged me, Sidney.

Sid   Yes, well, I'm sorry about that.

Barbara   It was my fault.

Sid   I forgive you. Let's go and get a cup of tea.

Barbara   I'll tell you what I think, Sidney. I think we're in danger here. I think we're in danger of having a horrible messy affair.

Sid   No no no . . .

Barbara   No, let me finish. I've been thinking about it all day and I've come to a decision. And I warn you, Sid, my decisions are final.

Sid   Don't say that.

Barbara   No, I've decided.

Sid   No, please, girl . . .

Barbara   I think we should get it over with.

Sid   You what?

Barbara   Nothing permanent. Nothing public. One night of bliss and that's your lot. Take it or leave it.

Sid   I'll take it.

Barbara   Thought you might.

Sid   You mean it?

Barbara   I've been to bed with enough men I didn't like.

I suddenly seemed ridiculous to keep turning you down. Because I do like you, Sidney. I like you very much. I warn you though, if Ronnie finds out, we're both for the high jump.

Sid   Come here.

They move towards each other. We hear **Kenneth** *off.*

Kenneth   Mind your step, it's like the swamplands of the Matagasi round here . . .

Sid *glances through the window.*

Enter **Kenneth** *leading a huge, dangerous-looking man called* **Eddie**.

Eddie   I'm supposed to be keeping an eye on Mrs Knight, not nobbing it up with you lot. Ronnie reckons you lot get up to allsorts.

Kenneth   Yes, well that's a commonly held myth, you see. In actual fact we're all very familial.

Sid *glances through the window.*

Sid   Gawd, strewth. He's bringing him over!

Barbara   Who?

Sid   Eddie.

Barbara   Eddie? Oh, bloody hell; I don't want Eddie to find me here.

Eddie   There's nothing dodgy goes on then, like in Hollywood?

Kenneth   Good heavens no. We all keep ourselves to ourselves. That's why you must say hello to Sidney; he gets very lonely in his little van.

Barbara   Sod this for a game of soldiers.

Sid   What you doing?

Barbara   Hiding.

Sid   No!

Barbara   Ronnie's told him to look out for any hanky-panky.

Sid   Tell him we're working. Doing our lines. What's he going to think, we're sitting here, talking, fully dressed.

Sally *pops her head out, soap in her eyes.*

Sally   Is there a towel?

Sid   Oh Gawd, strewth.

Barbara   Oh, bloody hell; it's an orgy.

Sid   It's all perfectly innocent.

Barbara   That's not how it looks, Sid. And besides, it isn't, is it?

Sally   Towel, please!

Eddie   Hold on, Kenny, I've lost my shoe.

Kenneth   Where?

Eddie   It's behind me.

Kenneth   Hang on.

Sally   What's going on?

Barbara   Sally, do us a favour and keep quiet for five minutes, will you?

Sally   Why?

Sid   Because you haven't got your clothes on. And get your clothes on.

Sally   Which?

Sid   Which what?

Sally   I can't do both in here.

Sid   Keep quiet then.

Barbara   Please, Sally; or Ronnie'll do his nut.

Sally   This is ridiculous.

Barbara   Sally, please.

Sally   All right. Jesus.

Eddie   That's ruined that is. Ronnie got me these in Bond Street.

Kenneth   Nearly there now.

Barbara   I'll be in the bedroom.

Sid   No!

Barbara   Sidney!

Sid   That'll be the first place he looks. Hide in here.

He offers her the toilet.

Barbara   In there?!

Sid   Think of your health.

Barbara   I'm claustrophobic.

Sid   Think of mine then.

She hides. **Imogen** *appears from the bedroom.*

Imogen   I'm feeling a bit sick, actually . . .

Sid *closes the door on her.* **Eddie** *and* **Kenneth** *arrive.*

Kenneth   Anybody home?

Sid   I was just on my way out.

Kenneth   Oh, well then, lucky we caught you. May we *entré?* Oh, *quel surprise.* All on your ownsome. In you come, Eddie.

Sid   It's a bit inconvenient at the moment.

Kenneth   Don't be so inhospitable; he's got a soggy sock. Eddie's a big fan of yours, well, enormous in fact, as you can see.

Eddie   I'm pleased to meet you.

Sid   Mutual, I'm sure. Thing is I'm a bit um . . .

Kenneth Overwhelmed he is; he's always overwhelmed by public adoration, even in small dollops.

Sid Do you think we could . . .

Kenneth Can I have a lie-down?

Sid No.

Kenneth Why not?

Sid Well, it's a bit . . . inconvenient at the moment.

Kenneth Yes. Too inconvenient to sign his poor mother's book. That's all he wants you know; he wants you to sign your moniker in his poor old mother's book.

Eddie If you wouldn't mind.

Sid Sure. No problem. Who to?

Eddie My mother.

Sid What's her name?

Eddie Mum.

Sid Right. There.

Eddie Thanks.

Sid Pleasure.

Kenneth Have you seen Miss Windsor?

Sid Hardly ever.

Kenneth She's wanted on the set.

Eddie There is another thing.

Sid What's that?

Eddie Well . . . would you mind if I spoke to Mr James in private?

Kenneth Not at all. In fact, why don't you two sit down and have a nice long tête-à-tête?

Eddie No thanks; I've eaten.

Kenneth   I'll leave you to it. If you do see Miss Windsor, they're ready for her close-up and they're losing the light.

Sid   Why don't we all go to the bus?

Kenneth   No, it's much cosier in here. Nice and private. Take your time.

Sid   Kenny . . .

Kenneth   Best of British.

Kenneth *leaves, but hangs about the end of the van, listening.*

Eddie   I'm a bit embarrassed, tell you the truth, but Ronnie asked me to have a word in your ear.

Sid   A word?

Eddie   He asked me to ask you nicely if you'd got designs on his wife.

Sid   Designs? That's . . .

Eddie   Have you?

Sid   Have I what?

Eddie   Are you shaggin' his missus?

Sid   No. Absolutely not. Absolutely not at all.

Eddie   Thing is, you've got a bit of a reputation and Ronnie thought . . .

Sid   Well, you can tell Ronnie there is absolutely nothing to worry about.

Eddie   Thing is you hear all sorts of things about you lot.

Sid   Eddie. I can completely reassure you about this. All those stories about showbiz antics are a complete myth. Me and Mrs Knight are just fellow artistes, in fact we're barely friends, in actual fact I haven't set eyes on her in days.

Kenneth *has discovered the caravan is supported at one end with a dodgy pile of bricks. He gives the bricks a malicious kick. The caravan tips up to a wild angle, spilling* **Sid** *on to the divan.*

Barbara *falls out of the toilet and lands on top of him.* **Sally** *tumbles out of the shower, loses her towel, bounces off* **Eddie** *and lands on* **Sid** *and* **Barbara**. **Imogen** *flies in and lands on top of them all.* **Eddie** *manages to stay upright.*

Sid   And I'll tell you something else. This is the last time I share a dressing-room.

Blackout.

Act Three

The van stands in a pub car park. The curtains are drawn against a crisp spring day. **Sid** *is lying like a corpse in a seventeenth-century shift. He looks much older.* **Sally** *enters, draped with various bits of seventeenth-century costume. She sees* **Sid** *and looks at him curiously. It occurs to her he might be dead. Then* **Sid** *snores loudly and she relaxes. Her little fright galvanises a decision she's been trying to make. She rummages in her bag for a letter, and in her purse for a small rather crumpled photograph. She puts the photo in the envelope, seals it, and places it prominently where* **Sid** *usually sits. He wakes.*

Sid Whassat?

Sally It's me. Heath's resigned.

Sid Has he?

Sally Harold Wilson's gone to see the Queen.

Sid She will be pleased.

Sally It's a new era. A new beginning. There's some post for you.

Sid Bin it.

Sally No. I'm not going to bin it any more.

Sid *picks up the letter.*

Sid It'll be from that mad nun in Shrewsbury.

Sally You don't know who it's from, so read it.

Sid *discards the letter.* **Sally** *begins dressing a female blonde wig.*

Sally I've been offered a job.

Sid That's nice.

Sally I've been offered a job on James Bond.

Enter **Kenneth**.

Kenneth   There's been something of a discussion at lunch and it has fallen to me on behalf of your fellow cast and the entire crew to make you cogniscent of the fact that you're behaving like a lovesick teenage imbecile.

Sally   Leave him alone, Kenny.

Kenneth   We're of a single mind that the sooner you two put an end to this ludicrous affair, the better.

Sally   Kenneth, please. He's not well.

Sid   I'm perfectly all right.

Sally   Oh, please yourself!

Sally *leaves*.

Kenneth   This thing is affecting the morale of the entire unit.

Sid   What morale?

Kenneth   You were never good for morale. When Phil Silvers stood in for you there was better morale.

Sid   You all hated Phil Silvers.

Kenneth   Exactly; and it was great for morale! Whereas your partial return to health has had entirely the opposite effect. Behind the crapulent scenery as well as in front.

Sid   Have you heard something?

Kenneth   What about?

Sid   Don't mess me about, Kenneth. Have you heard any rumours?

Kenneth   I don't know what you mean, I'm sure.

Sid   Are they gonna drop me?

Kenneth   Well, it's about time.

Sid   That's very supportive of you.

Kenneth   Yes, well, I wouldn't worry. Peter won't.

Sid   Gerald wants to.

Kenneth   Ignore 'em. It's just the usual bollocks. Put the fear of God into us and keep the money down.
Sid   When they got rid of Charlie . . .

Kenneth   They didn't get rid of Charlie. Charlie got rid of himself. Charlie was so full of lemonade he couldn't perambulate let alone articulate.

Sid   But what have you heard?

Kenneth   Only the patently obvious. That your battered old mug running around leering up skirts and God help me snogging girls half your age is no longer the side-splitting sight it used to be.

Sid   I know.

Kenneth   There comes a time in every man's life he can no longer lech without appearing something of a dirty old sod. A benchmark you passed in the late nineteen fifties.

Sid   I know.

Kenneth   The sight of your face near a heaving bosom is positively excruciating.

Sid   I know.

Kenneth   You've got a very grubby image.

Sid   All right, all right; don't rub it in. That's why I took the sitcom. Family man.

Kenneth   Tip of the week; when you're playing her dad, don't think about Sally Geeson's bum.

Sid   I never look at her bum. I never look anywhere near her bum.

Kenneth   Yes, that's how I knew you were thinking about it. The boy's nice.

Sid   Robin? He's a good lad. I've got him a part in this.

Kenneth   You want to watch your back. He reminds me

of you when you were younger.

Sid   Oh, fuck 'em.

Kenneth   This is my last, anyway. Positively my last. I said I'd only do it if they cut the stocks scene; I'm not being pelted with rubbish at my age.

Sid   Stocks scene's still in.

Kenneth   It is not.

Sid   It's on the call sheet.

Kenneth   Oh no it isn't.

Sid   Stoke Poges. Tuesday. Scene 97. Captain Fancy. Villagers and Yokels. Construction erect stocks.

Kenneth   What day is it?

Sid   Tuesday.

Kenneth   Give me the phone. I've had enough of this duplicity. They think they can get away with blue murder. I can't look at a tomato without breaking out. It'll play havoc with me skin and I've got the Cabaret on Sunday. (*Phone.*) This is Kenneth Williams. Is Peter there? Yes, he's always out to lunch, isn't he. Well, you can tell him from me, he'd better get his obese old backside down to the set because I categorically refuse to be humiliated any further.

Sid   You'll do it, mate.

Kenneth   I will not.

Sid   If you don't, they won't use you next time.

Kenneth   Well, that'll be a blessing.

Sid   Are they going to drop me?

Kenneth   Way things are going they won't have to. Let's face it; the whole things running out of steam. Rothwell's had it. I'm getting gags the third time round. Windsor's doing another flash. I sometimes think we should all just grow up.

Barbara *enters. She's not happy.*

Barbara I thought you'd be in here. I saw you all, gossiping in the bus.

Kenneth We were not gossiping, we were having a compassionate discussion ...

Barbara My arse. I can fight my own battles thank you very much.

Sid I hope you've calmed down.

Barbara Yes, I've calmed down. This is me calmed down, all right? Is this calm enough for you?

Sid Kenny; sling your hook.

Barbara No, Kenny; stay where you are.

Sid You want to talk in front of him?

Barbara I don't want you jumping me.

Sid When have I ever done that?

Kenneth I could stand by with a bucket of water.

Sid You'll stand by with a thick ear in a minute.

Kenneth Sexaholic.

Sid Shirt-lifter.

Kenneth Dick.

Sid Bum bandit.

Kenneth South African.

Sid How dare you.

Barbara Will you stop it! You're as pathetic as each other.

Kenneth That is a slur. I do not feel the necessity to wield my penis in the pursuit of dominance. My ego is not hostage to my gonads. Women exist for me to bitch with or bitch about or bitch about with, not to satisfy an addled libido.

Sid   And how's your mother?

Kenneth   Irrelevant.

Sid   Domineering mother plus weak or absent father equals poofta, mate. It's common knowledge.

Barbara   Sid; we have to talk.

Kenneth   Well, if it's psychology you want; what about six-year-old boy gets dumped by mother who buggers off to Australia as one half of a comedy dance duo, and grows up a misogynist comedian who only fancies younger women and argues incessantly with Joan Sims?

Sid   Very perceptive. Who was it had to beg the Best Boy not to tell his mother what he'd been up to behind the honey wagon?

Barbara   Look, will you both stop it!

Sid   It's unnatural for a man to fancy other men!

Barbara   Kenny doesn't fancy other men. He fancies himself. Other men are just the next best thing.

Sally *enters.*

Sally   Kenny; you're wanted on set. Scene 97.

Kenneth   Right. It's about time they learned they can't muck me about. The final showdown. *Finito. La fin.* And you watch your steaming great gob or I'll do you for slander.

Sid   Slander, you couldn't do the Marquis de Sade for slander, mate!

Exit **Kenneth.**

Sally   Sid, they're gonna want you in your frock.

Sid   Oh, bollocks.

Sally   It's a lovely colour.

Sid   I hate drag.

Sally   Be a brave soldier.

Sid   It's all right; I'll do it.

Sally   Do you know how to get into it?

Barbara   Yes, he does.

Sally   Hurry up then.

Sally *leaves.* **Sid** *changes costume.*

Barbara   And when you're dressed, the first thing you're gonna do is apologise to Bernie.

Sid   All I said to Bernie was . . .

Barbara   All he was doing was helping me off a horse.

Sid   He was taking liberties.

Barbara   Hairy bloody great thing.

Sid   He is an' all.

Barbara   Not Bernie; the horse! He was helping me down.

Sid   He was touching you up.

Barbara   I hate horses.

Sid   Lecherous sod.

Barbara   I'd told him I hated horses.

Sid   You never told me you hated horses.

Barbara   You never bleeding asked.

Sid   Well, if you don't like horses you shouldn't be on a horse. You shouldn't have let them put you on a horse.

Barbara   Sidney.

Sid   He had his hand on your bottom. You don't need to put your hand on someone's bottom to help them off a horse.

Barbara   You don't need to put your tongue in someone's ear to wish them Merry Christmas, but it's never stopped you. Scenes with a horse are a doddle compared to scenes with you. I've seen you do ten lines of dialogue juggling half a dozen props and hit your mark for the sight gag with no rehearsal in one bloody take. But give you the feed and me on your knee freezing my tits off in underwear and no; we're there for two and a half hours. Talk to me about groping and it's not Bernie springs to mind. Talk about gentlemanly conduct and you're talking Bernie. Talk to me about trying to act with another actor taking personal liberties and it's you. It's you I think of. It's you who's happy to humiliate me in front of the entire crew.

Sid   I don't like that sort of scene any more than you.

Barbara   It was ghastly. I felt sick and degraded.

Sid   I have never treated you with disrespect.

Barbara   I know a real kiss when I get one.

Sid   It was scripted.

Barbara   It was meant. It was embarrassing.

Sid   It was a kiss. A kiss is a kiss.

Barbara   And work is work.

Sid   What about Brighton?

Barbara   What about it?

Sid   I don't recall a camera.

Barbara   Brighton was Brighton.

Sid   Was it that much of a disaster?

Barbara   It wasn't a disaster, it was . . .

Sid   Well, what was it?

Barbara   I just wanted to get it over with. I wanted you to get it out of your system. I thought you just wanted to give me one; wallop.

Sid   Well, that's a terrible thing to think.

Barbara   Sidney, I'm thirty years younger than you, we're both married, we're both unfaithful; it doesn't exactly augur well, does it?

Sid   You're gonna have to leave him now, you know.

Barbara   I'm not leaving him.

Sid   You said you were going to.

Barbara   No I didn't.

Sid   You did. You said you'd had enough.

Barbara   That was about him and me, not you and me.

Sid   I'm leaving mine.

Barbara   Sidney . . .

Sid   No, enough's enough.

Barbara   You can't leave Val.

Sid   Why not?

Barbara   Because you love her. And you love your kids. I've seen you with them.

Sid   It's not about Val.

Barbara   How do you think I'd feel, imagining Val? Sitting on her own in Iver? If it wasn't for her you'd be skint, drunk and unemployed. Whatever happened to whatsisname.

Sid   I know. I'm not denying it.

Barbara   Well then.

Sid   I reckon I've got a good ten years left in me. And I want to spend them with you.

Barbara   Oh great. I get your last ten years, then a few more mopping up after you, and then what? I'm high and dry at forty.

Sid   In Brighton you said . . .

Barbara   Will you leave off about bloody Brighton?

Sid   Didn't you enjoy it?

Barbara   The foreplay especially. Forty-five minutes drinking warm champagne and waiting for Val to phone.

Sid   I know the earth didn't exactly move.

Barbara   I'm not going to massage your ego, Sid. Look where it's got me so far. You don't want me; it's the *idea* of me you want.

He hands her a chit.

Barbara   What's this?

Sid   It's a doctor's certificate.

Barbara   What for?

Sid   Fit as a fiddle.

Barbara   I don't want to see your doctor's certificate.

Sid   You said you were worried about me ticker. Me ticker's fine.

Barbara   Sidney.

Sid   There it is in black and white.

Barbara   Oh my God.

Sid   What's in Stanmore anyway? You said yourself you never see him. A Merc in the drive . . .

Barbara   A Daimler.

Sid   A Daimler in the drive . . .

Barbara   The Merc's in the garage . . .

Sid   A Merc in the garage . . .

Barbara   Next to the Jag.

Sid   But apart from the motors, what is there in Stanmore?

Barbara   About two hundred thousand in used notes. And a marriage, Sidney.

Sally *enters.*

Sally   Barbara, they're ready for you.

Barbara   My marriage.

Barbara *leaves.*

Sally   Kenny's being difficult; you may as well relax.

Sid *pours a drink.*

Sally   Read your letter.

Sid   I can't. I've got that double vision thing again.

Sally   I wish you'd stop drinking.

Sid   Read it to me.

Sally   No. It's addressed to you.

Sid   Chuck it then.

Sally   All right; I'll read it. I'm opening it. Oh there's a photo.

Sid   Is it a nun?

Sally   No.

Sid   Bin it.

Sally   No.

Sid   Oh . . . read it then.

Sally   'Dear Sidney James.'

Sid   Read it quietly.

Sally   'Dear Sidney James. It's been hard to decide if I should contact you or not, but as you can see I have decided to write. The photo enclosed is of someone you will recognise. It is a picture of my mother. Her name was

Jenny, her maiden name was Barlow. You'll remember her as one half of Heaven on Wheels, the speciality act with which you toured the Midlands in 1944.'

Sid That's enough.

Sally There's more.

Sid I wouldn't be surprised.

Sally 'You were performing as Max Miller at the time, and suggested she join with you to rehearse a short tap routine. Sadly, the routine never saw the light of day, but rehearsals went on throughout the tour. My mother always believed I was conceived in Wolverhampton, but not that you had any knowledge of my subsequent arrival. Shortly after the tour ended she was suprised to learn of your sudden marriage. Rather than cause any trouble, she chose to marry an old admirer, a solicitor from Berkshire. My stepfather's generosity towards her did not, sadly, extend to myself, and as I grew so did a degree of bitterness between them. They divorced when I was six years old, and my mother brought me up alone. She died ten years ago of a miserable cancer. Sorting through her things I came apon her diaries and some photographs. It was not hard to deduce my true parentage. It's only after a great deal of thought that I'm writing to you. I want you to understand I want nothing from you, but I do want to meet you. I want you to know me. I want to talk to you about my mother.

Sid That's enough.

Sally To hear that you remember her with affection would mean a great deal to me . . .'

Sid I said that's enough.

Sally There's a picture.

Sid Bin it.

Sally A picture of her mother.

Sid Sally. If it happened in the mid-nineteen forties, I don't remember it. It's water under the bridge. She's got her life, I've got mine.

Sally   What if she hasn't?

Sid   What?

Sally   Got a life?

Sid   Well, she should get one. I think I'll just take another little nap.

He lies back, closes his eyes.

Sally   Do you remember her?

Sid   God, I'm tired.

Sally   She's wearing her skates. Do you?

Sid   What?

Sally   Remember her?

Sid   Of course I do. She used to whizz round. Hopeless bloody hoofer, though.

Sally   Look.

Sid   No.

Sally   Look at her.

Sid   No.

Sally   But . . .

Sid   Sally, I'm knackered. Please. I need a kip.

Sally, *subdued, carefully puts the photo in her cardigan pocket. The corners of her mouth start to dip down in reflex misery. She is trying hard not to cry when the door opens and* **Eddie** *enters.* **Sally** *turns her back to hide her state and* **Eddie** *takes out a gun.* **Sally** *turns to see it, and is silenced by a single finger to the lips. She crumples backwards in surprise. He cocks the gun and points it at* **Sid**'s *knee.* **Sally** *gurgles incoherently.*

Eddie   Wake up, Sidney.

Sid *opens his eyes and is suddenly very awake.*

Eddie I've got a message from Ron.

Sid Have you? That's nice.

Eddie He told me to tell you it's not so much the money, and it's not so much you shagging his wife, it's more you shagging his wife when you owe him so much money. He feels that's taking the piss somewhat.

Sid I hadn't thought about it quite like that, but on reflection he's absolutely right.

Eddie I told him you've got a dodgy ticker, so he told me be sure not to frighten you too much.

Sid How much is too much?

Eddie Bit more than not enough, I suppose.

Sid Well, I'd say you've done a bit more than not enough, hovering on the much more, which is dangerously close to too much, wouldn't you say?

Sally Please; leave him alone.

Eddie It's all right love, I'm not going to hurt him. Ronnie was very particular about that. Don't want you to have a heart attack, do we?

Sid That's very kind. I'll try not to.

Eddie Ron said I shouldn't bring a shooter or nothing 'cos if I did you might.

Sid I might, yes. It's a distinct possibility.

Eddie That's what I thought. So I said I wouldn't fire it.

Sid Good idea.

Eddie He's very fond of you.

Sid · Is he?

Eddie Compared to the other arty farties she hangs out with, he loves you.

Sid   Me too; it's mutual.

Eddie   I can never get over how much bigger you look on the telly.

Sid   I'm ... usually standing up.

Eddie   I think I'll pull the trigger after all.

Sid   No, no. Don't.

Sally   No please, don't.

Sid   I wouldn't if I were you.

Eddie   Just don't have a heart attack, all right?

Sid   Well, I'm not sure I can guarantee that.

Sally   *Please* don't.

Sid   In fact I think it just missed a beat.

Eddie   You little fibber.

Sid   No, definitely.

Eddie *releases the safety catch.*

Sally   Ahh!

Sid   Ooh; there it goes again.

Eddie   Now, watch. Watch!

Sid   No.

Eddie   No, don't close your eyes; watch.

Sid   I should cocoa.

Eddie   I'm not going to do it if you don't open your eyes.

Sid   I'm not bloody gonna then.

Eddie   Open your eyes.

Sally   Don't make him open his eyes!

Eddie   Open your eyes or the girl gets it.

Sally   Open your eyes! Sid, open your eyes.

Sid   All right! My eyes are open. Look. Open eyes. My eyes are wide open, only please; let's talk about this.

Eddie   Just watch. And don't tell Ron.

Sally   No!

Sid *whimpers. A little flag with BANG on it pops out of the gun.*

Sid   Ahhh! Euhhh. Ohh. Mm.

Eddie *laughs.*

Sally   You bastard.

Eddie   That's good, innit? I got that from Alan Alan.

Sally   You complete bastard!

Sid   Agh.

Eddie   You all right?

Sid   Fine . . . .

Sid *gets pains down his arm and gesticulates.*

Sally   Oh, Jesus.

Eddie   What does he want?

Sally   He wants his tablets.

Eddie   His what?

Sally   His nitroglycerine.

Eddie   What? Oh, no. Now listen. Listen to me. You are NOT having a heart attack, all right!

Sid *can't breath.*

Eddie   Did you hear me! Give him his fucking tablets! Listen, you ponce; if you have a bleeding heart attack I *will* fucking shoot you. You listening to me? Sid? Please don't have a heart attack. Please? Please don't. It's not a real gun, Sid. Look. It's for kids. I was thinking; they shouldn't sell them to kids really. Could have someone's eye out with that. Listen, Sid, don't die, mate. Please? Ron'll fucking kill me.

Sid Go away.

Eddie You all right?

Sid Never better.

Sally I'll get a doctor.

Sid No! Stop fussing.

Sally That was your last one.

Sid There's another bottle in the car, in the glove compartment.

Sally *leaps up.*

Sally You could have killed him.

Eddie No, be fair.

Sally You stupid bloody animal.

Eddie It would have been strictly unintentional.

Sally You should be locked up.

Exit **Sally**.

Eddie She's not entirely alone in that opinion. It breeds prejudice, this profession. People tend to forget we're all individuals. Ronnie didn't want to hurt you. Dampen his ardour; that's what he said. Is your ardour dampened?

Sid Sopping.

Eddie Right then. Anyway; he sends his love.

Sid That's nice of him.

Eddie He's a nice bloke.

Sid He's a diamond.

Enter **Kenneth**, *covered in tomatoes and assorted rotten grocery,* **Barbara** *bringing up the rear.*

Kenneth Don't look at me. Don't speak to me. I have

never been so humiliated in my life.

Barbara   Don't bang on about it, Kenny; it's only fruit and veg.

Kenneth   Oh, the filth. The disease!

Barbara   I've never seen walk-ons so enthusiastic.

Kenneth   Poxy Middlesex wankers.

Barbara   There was a fight for the fruit between them and the props boys. Hello, Eddie. What are you doing here?

Kenneth   Get me to the shower. Cleanse me immediately.

Barbara   Oh, get in there and cleanse yourself. What do you want, Eddie?

Eddie   Ronnie asked me to come and have a little chat with Sid.

Barbara   Oh, he did, did he.

Kenneth   This has made me mind up. There's going to be no more of this. This is absolutely the last one. I'd rather do *Call My Bluff*.

Exit **Kenneth** *to the shower. Enter* **Sally** *with tablets.* **Sid** *takes a couple more.*

Sally   Here.

Barbara   Are you all right?

Sid   I'm fine, for Christ's sake.

Barbara   Eddie, he's not well!

Eddie   No, he's fine. Aren't you, Sid?

Sally   Could you get the hell out of here please!

Eddie   Manners.

Sally   There's some other gorilla over in the car park come looking for you.

Eddie   Yeh?

Barbara   Sounds like Charlie.

Eddie   Looking for me?

Barbara   Ronnie must want you for some other little errand. Go on then.

Eddie   Right. Keep it damp, Sid.

Eddie *leaves.*

Sally   Twenty-seven's next. Shall I get Peter to reschedule?

Sid   No.

Barbara   How are you feeling?

Sid   Stop fussing, will you.

Sally   I'm going to call a doctor.

Sid   No.

Barbara   I think she should Sid.

Sid   I'm fine.

Sally   I'll phone from the pub.

Sally *leaves.*

Sid   I'm going to be needed soon.

Barbara   Let's be on the safe side, shall we?

Sid   Just leave it alone. I'm fine.

Barbara   Oh, Sidney. What am I going to do with you?

Sid   Take me home.

Barbara   Oh, right. Yours or mine?

Sid   I just want to go home of an evening and find you there.

Barbara   Sid, you have to stop this.

Sid   Tell me I'm wrong.

Barbara   This is making you ill. You look lovely.

Sid   Don't start.

Barbara   Where's your sense of humour?

Sid   In my trouser pocket. Let's get a place of our own.

Barbara   People would laugh, Sid. People would laugh at us.

Sid   No they wouldn't.

Barbara   I think they would.

Sid   Well, it's a living.

Barbara   Behind our backs.

Sid   Let 'em. I don't care.

Barbara   Well I do. I've been a joke too much of my life. I don't want my private life public; I don't want to be laughed at, I don't want to be pitied, I want to lock my door at night and leave Her outside.

Sid   Leave her in Stanmore. We'll get our own place.

Barbara   Sid, when you look at me you don't see me you see Her. So when I look at you I see Her in your eyes. I try to be me when I'm with you but I'm not. She's there between us. And He's between us too; good old Sid. Yuck yuck yuck. When I'm with you, Sid, I don't know who the fuck I am.

Sid   You are the finest woman I ever set eyes on. The noblest, the brightest, the kindest. You could make my entire life worth living.

They gaze into each other's eyes.

I mean it.

Barbara   I know you do.

She leans forward to kiss him, and **Eddie** *enters.*

Eddie Mrs K. Ronnie's got a little problem.

Barbara What sort of little problem?

Eddie He's been arrested.

Barbara He's been what?

Eddie Banged up.

Barbara What for?

Sid Nothing trivial, I hope?

Eddie Suspicion of murder.

Barbara What?

Sid You're joking.

Barbara That's ridiculous.

Eddie I know.

Barbara He's not that sort of bloke.

Eddie He *knows* that sort of bloke.

Barbara But he's not one of 'em.

Eddie I know.

Sid Who got murdered?

Eddie Some Italian geezer.

Barbara Zamperelli?

Eddie Yep.

Barbara Oh, Jesus.

Sid Why would Ronnie murder an Italian?

Barbara He didn't.

Eddie He wouldn't.

Sid I know; he never would. So why'd they arrest him?

Eddie   The Italian murdered Ronnie's brother.

Sid   I see.

Eddie   Lucky for him Ronnie's not like that.

Sid   Absolutely. He's dead though?

Eddie   He is. And Ronnie's a bit pissed off, I can tell you.

Barbara   I bloody knew it. I knew they'd pick up Ronnie.

Sid   You sure he didn't do it?

Barbara   I know he didn't.

Sid   Were you with him?

Barbara   No, as a matter of fact I was with you.

Eddie   He says you're to get to Hendon nick straight away.

Barbara   Tell the stupid bastard I'm working.

Eddie   He was very insistent.

Barbara   Tell him he can go to hell. I told him not to threaten Zamperelli. Tell him I bloody warned him.

Eddie   He won't like it.

Barbara   Go on, Eddie; get gone.

Eddie   Couldn't I tell him you love him and you'll stick by him no matter what?

Barbara   No, Eddie, you stick by him. You tell him you love him.

Eddie   Well, I'll give it a try.

Barbara   Goodbye, Eddie.

Eddie   Bye then.

She's ushered him out.

Barbara   Oh, sod him.

Sid   It's a sign, this is.

Barbara   Sod him, sod him, sod him.

Sid   It's fate, that's what it is.

Barbara   What am I going to do?

Sid   Well, you can stop worrying for a start. He's made his bed and he can lie in it. You can get on with your life. You know what I fancy?

He gets out a bottle of champagne.

Barbara   I don't know what to do.

Sid   It'll all turn out for the best. You'll see. It's all gonna be hunky-dory. End of the shoot, you and me, Capri. Or a Cortina down to Camber Sands. Come on, we'll have the time of our lives.

She suddenly runs out of the caravan.

Barbara   Eddie!

Eddie (*off*)   Yeh?

Barbara   Tell him I love him.

Eddie (*off*)   That's more like it.

Barbara   Tell him I'll be there as soon as I can. Eddie! And for as long as it takes.

Eddie (*off*)   Right. I will.

She returns to the van.

Sid   How long's that then?

Barbara   How long's what?

Sid   As long as it takes?

Barbara   Depends what they think they've got on him. Days. God help him, months.

Sid   What if he goes down?

Barbara He won't go down.

Sid What if he does?

Barbara He won't.

Sid He might. What if he does?

Barbara We'll appeal.

Sid That could take years.

Barbara Well, that's what I mean, that's what it means. As long as it takes.

Sid I'm fifty-nine.

Barbara You're sixty-one.

Sid You see?

A terrible pause. She sees the champagne bottle he still holds.

Barbara You selfish sod.

Sid Yeah but . . .

Barbara You fuck.

Sid No listen . . .

Barbara Don't say it, Sidney. Whatever it is don't even think it.

Sid He's a villain! He's a useless waste of ruddy space.

Barbara He's my husband.

Sid Yeah but why him? Why choose him? Why has it always been, why does it have to be *him*?

Barbara Because there's a bit of me Ronnie holds in trust, in perpetuity. The me he looks after is the me that's me. The me I recognise. I can come home to him and there I am.

Sid You can't if he's in bloody Wandsworth.

Barbara That's not the point. The point is, whether you like it or not you belong with Val. You belong to her.

Sid No, no no.

Barbara Yes. Like a coat on a hook. If it's cold out, you want your coat; you know where it is. You want reminding who you are; you know who to go to. That's love, isn't it?

Sid *is suddenly near to tears. He bites his hand.*

Barbara Isn't it?

Sid (*hardly audible*) But I don't like him.

Barbara What?

Sid I don't like him.

Barbara Ronnie?

Sid No. The bloke I am when I'm with Val. I don't like him any more.

Barbara Well, that's very sad. There are times I could strangle Ronnie, but the me that's there with him is always the me I love.

Sid Well, this is the me I love. The me you're looking at.

Barbara What about when you're alone, Sid; do you love him then? Well that's very sad Sidney, because it's not going to work. All this desire; it's just self-pity.

Sid Please, girl . . .

Barbara This is the thing, Sid. This is what it is. This is the problem. You used to make me laugh. That was a long time ago. You don't make me laugh any more. You make me unhappy. Being with you makes me unhappy. Your wanting me makes me unhappy. I'm unhappy because you're unhappy and you're unhappy because of me. That's a whole lifetime of unhappiness piling up around us unless one of us has the strength to give it up.

Sid I can't live without you. I'm not sure I can. I'm getting old. I'm worn out. I'm wearing out. My back aches. This eye's all blurred every morning. I've had a cough since 1969. Nothing heals any more. I don't want to get old.

Barbara   I can't stop you getting old, Sid. If we were together I wouldn't be new any more. And all you ever want is someone new. If you feel old Sid, it's because all you dream of is new.

Barbara *kisses his knuckles and leaves.*
Kenneth *returns silently, towelling his hair.*

Kenneth   Yes, well. That's better. No good sitting there covered in muck; you want to give yourself a good hose down. I came to see you last month, at the Victoria Palace. I didn't come round. Sitting in the circle being force-fed that peurile tat was bad enough. I don't blame you; it's the same swill we've all been slopping about in for years. You were dreadful. And you know it. So was everyone else. Except her. She was doing her Marie Lloyd and suddenly I heard heavy breathing over my shoulder. I thought I know that wheeze. It was you, breathless, leaning on the back of the circle. It's a big place, Victoria Palace. I thought, if he's up and down those stairs twice nightly just for a gawp at madam he's not long for this world. [Mind you,] the saddest thing was the audience. They weren't even in with a chance of a fumble. All they could do was watch. Then at the curtain call you came forward and said 'Did you like it?' And they all shouted 'Yes!' and you said 'Good, 'cos we're going to do the whole ruddy thing over again' and I thought God help us, that's all we've ever done.

Sid *drinks.*

Kenneth   You know why you love her, Sid? She's vivid. From the Greek. Vivace. She's vivacious; and she vivifies. She pertains to life. She's somehow got the hang of it, unlike us.

Sid *bows his head.* **Kenneth**, *in an unthinking moment of compassion, touches the back of* **Sid**'s *head.* **Sid**, *surprised, flinches. Stares at him aggressively.* **Kenneth** *backs off.* **Sally** *enters.*

Sally   Your GP's on a housecall and the Slough ambulance is on strike and do we want one from Hammersmith and have you actually collapsed and I said no and they said well find out if you had and phone them back.

Kenneth   He's all right. Back to his old self.

Kenneth *leaves.*

Sally   Are you all right?

Sid *nods.*

Sally   Do you need another pill?

Sid *shakes his head.*

Sally   What's the matter?

Sid   She's gone.

Sally   Have another pill.

He brushes her off.

I don't want you to die!

Sid   I don't intend to.

Sally *takes out the photo.*

Sally   Look at her?

Sid   Why?

Sally   Please.

Sid   What for?

Sally   For me.

He takes the photo. Looks at it. Puts it down.

Sally   Well?

Sid   Well what?

Sally   Is it her?

Sid   Yes it's her. Jane.

Sally   Jenny.

Sid   You're right. Jenny with the two left feet. Don't look at me like that. It's just there's so many of you. Bin it.

Sally   She'll turn up one day. One of your misdemeanours'll walk right through that door.

Sid   God help me.

Sally   What would you do then?

Sid   I'd give her a cup of tea and her train fare home. Let me get some kip, will you?

Sally   What if she wanted to be part of your life?

Sid   No room.

Sally   You've room enough for all your women.

Sid   There's only one woman in my life. And she's not in my life.
He drinks a large shot.

Sally   They're going all over the world.

Sid   Would you do me a favour?

Sally   All over the world, I'd get to go.

Sid   Sally.

Sally   What?

Sid   Would you give me a kiss?

Sally   No.

Sid   Please.

Sally   I gave you a kiss.

Sid   That was years ago. Give us another.

Sally   You said one'd be enough.

Sid   One's never enough.

Sally   Singapore they're going. And Australia.

Sid   If you won't give us a kiss, undress for me.

Sally   No.

Sid   I won't touch you. Let me just . . . look.

Sally   No.

Sid   Please.

Sally   No.

Sid *begins to cry. It's a deep and rending sorrow.* **Sally** *is frozen, torn between surprise and compassion.*

Sally   It's alright.

She touches him. He takes her face between his hands and kisses her. She pushes him away. Her mind is suddenly made up. She swiftly goes around the caravan collecting her things. She puts on her coat, grabs her bag, and goes to the door.

Sally   I'll send you a card.

The lights fade.

Act Four

Emmanuelle. 1978.

The caravan sits disused in a scrappy corner of Pinewood Studios, leaning at a permanent slant. The tatty curtains are pulled shut, the room dank and cold. It's raining outside. **Barbara** *stands just inside the door, just looking.* **Kenneth** *enters with a raincoat round his head and two plastic cups of tea.*

Kenneth I thought I'd find you here.

Barbara Oh, Kenny, don't get wet.

Kenneth A little late, alas.

Barbara Mind your step, it's all skew-wif.

Kenneth Brought you a cuppa.

Barbara Oh, ta.

Kenneth *enters the van.*

Kenneth Oh dear.

Barbara The rain's got in.

Kenneth Well, it's had it, hasn't it?

Barbara They shouldn't have let it rot.

Kenneth They should have given it to me.

Barbara They should have towed it away.

Kenneth I think they took your point. Peter summoned the site manager as soon as we finished the read-through.

Barbara How was it?

Kenneth We struggled through without you.

Barbara I couldn't face it.

Kenneth I'm not surprised.

Barbara   I knew it was only a cameo, I knew it wouldn't be much . . .

Kenneth   I know.

Barbara   I didn't want to *do* much . . .

Kenneth   Me neither.

Barbara   Then I flicked through to my scene, took one look at it, and I thought, oh no.

Kenneth   They think you've flounced off home.

Barbara   I went to the bar. Thought I'd come for one last look.

Kenneth   Nice to see you anyway, however briefly. How's Stanmore?

Barbara   Ronnie's gone.

Kenneth   Well, good riddance.

Barbara   Don't be flippant, Kenny, nothing's that simple. Years ago, when he was on remand he used to say to me; 'I can't do life. Life's a bleeding long time.' It is 'n all.

Kenneth   And just when you've had enough of it you've got your sixties to get through and your seventies to look forward too.

Barbara   Except Sid.

Kenneth   No. No seventies for Sid. Lucky swine.

Barbara   Oh, poor Sid. I miss him.

Kenneth   And poor Imogen.

Barbara   Oh, and Imogen. Why would anyone do that to themselves? Anyone as beautiful as that.

Sid's *playing cards are on the table.* **Barbara** *toys with them.*

Kenneth   She was thirty-eight and she didn't like herself. You're the only person I know who likes themselves. The rest of us grieve. We grieve for the person we dreamed of being but never grew into.

Barbara   Oh, cheer up. What's the rest of the script like?

Kenneth   Positively vile. It wasn't a read-through, it was a wade-through. One long relentless stream of badly written jokes cobbled together with disdain for the actors and complete contempt for the audience. One of the most morally and aesthetically offensive pieces of work I've ever read. I think I'll just camp it up.

Barbara   That's what I admire about you, Kenny; always searching for an original approach.

Kenneth   You've quit then?

Barbara   I don't want to get my tits out again, not for a naff cameo, not at my age.

Kenneth   They all had 'em out in *England.* Jack said he couldn't look anyone in the eye. I blame Robin Askwith's bottom.

Barbara   They're desperate.

Kenneth   I've got to get mine out in this.

Barbara   Really desperate. How is your bum?

Kenneth   Ask the Spanish inquisition; they seem to have taken up permanent residence. Desperate's not the word.

Barbara   You all got your botties out in *Constable.*

Kenneth   That was in context. And I was younger then. Do us a favour.

Barbara   What?

Kenneth   Will you have a butcher's?

Barbara   At what?

Kenneth   From a medical perspective?

Barbara   Kenneth!

Kenneth   I tried in the mirror, but I couldn't see a thing.

Then I pulled a muscle. I can't just walk into make-up. I fear I may have cultivated a small vineyard down there.

Barbara   Oh, please.

Kenneth   Have a look.

Barbara   No.

Kenneth   Fifteen years we've known each other and you won't even take a quick peek at me anus.

Barbara   If that's your definition of friendship, I'm not surprised you haven't got any. It's all right for you anyway; people don't have any expectations of a bottom.

Kenneth   Oh, well, yes, I'm well aware that your twin contributions to world culture stand at an altogether higher echelon.

Barbara   Slightly lower lately.

Kenneth   You've never disappointed.

Barbara   How would you know? I've watched you in rushes; you always look away.

Kenneth   I do no such thing.

Barbara   The slightest threat of a bare boob and you put sugar in your tea even though you've finished your tea and you don't take sugar.

Kenneth   Don't talk such utter drivel.

Barbara   You're all mouth and no trousers.

Kenneth   I've haunted the fleshpots of Morocco and the wings of the Talk of the Town. I've encountered more bosoms than you could shake a stick at . . .

She lifts up her sweater. He stirs his tea.

Kenneth   Well, I'm the wrong man to ask anyway. Isn't there some sort of test you can do with a pencil?

Barbara   I've tried it. I got as far as six pencils, a ruler and a fountain pen, then I gave up.

Kenneth   Well, if you ever get tired of acting, you'd do well at W.H. Smith's.

Barbara   I don't want to be humiliated any more.

Kenneth   I've been clenching my buttocks all week, which is above and beyond the call of duty for a man with my afflictions.

Barbara   I've been doing press-ups.

Kenneth   Bet you never got your chin off the floor.

Barbara   I never got my chin *on* it.

They laugh.

Kenneth   Here we go then; Venus unveiled.

Barbara   Oh, Kenny, no.

Kenneth   No, fair do's. I want to walk on to that soundstage exuding confidence from every orifice.

Barbara   Oh, go on then; get it over with.

He bares his bum.

Kenneth   Well?

Barbara   Oh, it's . . .

Kenneth   What?

Barbara   It's fine.

Kenneth   Fine?

Barbara   As bottoms go.

Kenneth   I know how bottoms go; that's what I'm worried about.

Barbara   Put it away.

Kenneth   Would you say it was perky?

Barbara   Not exactly.

Kenneth   Amusing?

Barbara   Well . . .

Kenneth   It's gruesome, isn't it?

Sally   Toupee tape.

Barbara   Ahh!

Kenneth   God in heaven!

Sally *appears from the shadows.*

Sally   Sorry.

Barbara   Oh. You frightened the life out of me.

Sally   Sorry.

Barbara   Where'd you come from?

Sally   I heard you coming so I sort of hid. Sorry. I thought you'd just pop in and go out again. You could use toupee tape. To lift the buttocks?

Kenneth   Yes. This was a private consultation. Thank you.

Barbara   What are you doing here?

Sally   Nothing. Same as you.

Barbara   What's that?

Sally   Remembering.

Barbara   You were close to Sid, weren't you? I always thought that.

Sally *gathers up the playing cards, places them tidily.*

Barbara   You didn't come to funeral. I remember being surprised you weren't there.

Sally   I was in Sunderland.

Barbara   Sunderland?

Sally   I wanted to see where he died. It's a huge theatre. I expected it to be closed but it wasn't. So I bought a ticket. It was a different show of course. It had that bloke from *On The Buses* in it. And a big fish-tank with some naked girls swimming in it. Sid would have liked that.

Barbara You should have come to the funeral.

Sally I went to Sunderland.

Kenneth How was the show?

Barbara Kenneth.

Sally Dreadful.

Kenneth Well, miss him if you must, but don't mourn for the manner of his passing. He died laughing at his own jokes, which was perfectly apt.

Barbara Have some compassion, Kenny. He worked himself to death.

Kenneth A number one tour of the provinces is too long and lingering a suicide, even for Sid to contemplate.

Barbara It was the drink then.

Kenneth I shouldn't think so. He could have entered his liver in the Olympics.

Barbara Well then what?!

Kenneth He had a heart attack, dearie. He was probably humping the ASM.

Barbara I should have called him back. He called me half a dozen times and I never called him back.

Kenneth Everything ends in silence. It has to be someone's. No love affair lasts for ever.

Sally Sid managed it.

Barbara What do you mean?

Sally It was for ever for Sid.

Barbara Don't.

Sally I'm glad for him.

Barbara   Do you believe in heaven?

Kenneth   You're no doubt expecting a cynical retort, but .
yes I do, as a matter of fact.

Barbara   What's it like, do you think?

Kenneth   It's whatever you most fancy.

Barbara   It's not lounging about on a cloud with angels
in togas, then?

Kenneth   Well, in my case that's just about spot on.
They'd have to be lewd little angels, though. I imagine a
banqueting table piled high with whatever you never got
enough of. One long eternal Roman orgy.

Barbara   You're so deep. I think heaven's being left
alone with a Steenbeck in the edit suite. You sit in front of
your life and you're allowed to re-edit it. Cut the rotten
bits, loop the good sex, montage the highlights . . . watch it
over and over. Live it again and again, a bit better every
time. And eventually . . . make it perfect. What about you,
Sally?

Sally   I don't believe in heaven.

Kenneth *feels the familiar nagging pain in his gut.*

Barbara   You all right?

He nods, in pain.

Barbara   Oh, Kenny.

Kenneth   Oh, I'm sick of this. I wish I could just retire,
jack it all in.

Barbara   Why don't you?

Kenneth   Because I'm a narcissistic nitwit, and the little
pond of my celebrity is the only source of water in this
desert of a life. I couldn't survive my flat night after night
if I wasn't on the telly. I just wish they'd leave my bottom
out of it.

Barbara   Toupee tape. Have you got some?

Sally *tries to find some in her bag.*

Kenneth They don't even like me any more. The public loathe me.

Barbara Don't be ridiculous. There are millions out there who just adore you.

Kenneth Yes, most of whom I seem to run into between my flat and the bus stop, all carrying two large carrier bags and a can of Special Brew.

Barbara It's brilliant for boobs. We got through six rolls on *Dick*. Drop 'em, Kenny.

Kenneth Do what?

Barbara Trousers down.

Kenneth Oh, this is ridiculous.

Barbara Little trick of the trade, that's all.

She tapes his buttocks up.

Kenneth It's hard to describe the abject horror of being recognised in the street by terminally ugly unwashed ignoramuses who think etiquette's an expensive catfood.

Barbara They love you.

Kenneth I don't want the love of the nation, it's unhygienic.

Barbara There.

Kenneth How is it?

Barbara Pretty as a picture.

Kenneth Oh yes.

Barbara Well, it's not quite a Michelangelo.

Kenneth As long as it's less of a Stanley Spencer.

Barbara It belongs in the British Museum, Kenny.

Kenneth Oooh yes, I should be a permanent feature.

Facing the door as you come in with an inscription on me buttocks; The End is Nigh.

They laugh. **Kenneth** *suffers sudden stabbing pains. He stops laughing.* **Barbara** *holds his hand. He grips her tight until the pain subsides.*

Barbara   All right?

Kenneth   Oh . . . what's the bloody point?

The pain subsides.

You know when I knew it was all over? I got home one night last year and turned on the Cabaret. It had been a wet Sunday; it hadn't gone well but it hadn't been disastrous. And I turned it on and I heard canned laughter. They'd smothered me in canned laughter. And I recognised it. It was the same tape they use for all the sitcoms. They use it on *Bless This House*. You can actually recognise individual morons in the audience cackling away like the living dead. I didn't know who to feel sorrier for, them or me. Them mindlessly guffawing through eternity or me slogging me guts out for laughs that weren't even mine. I realised with some horror they could well have been laughing at Sid. Then they started putting out the films diced up like stewing steak and I swear I felt like they'd done it to me. Chopped me up and laid me out on six different trays in the butcher's window to be gawped at by millions of idiot plebeians who think talent's a substance that oozes out of game-show hosts and can't even laugh for themselves. Then me kidneys appeared on the *Parkinson* show and I knew we'd had it. We're dead already, we just lack the good taste to lie down.

Kenneth *leaves.*

Barbara   Come on; I'll buy you a gin.

Sally   No thanks.

Barbara   You can't sit here. You'll get mildew.

Sally   I'll be fine.

Barbara You don't look fine.

Sally They're going to tow it away! It's all there is left and you told them to tow it away.

Barbara I'm sorry. Oh, sweetheart, I'm sorry.

Sally I couldn't get him out of my head. I tried for months I went to Sunderland I stood outside the house I went to the grave at Kilburn and I couldn't get him out until I came back here and I came in here and this is where I left him.

Barbara Shhh.

Sally And you told them to tow it away.

Barbara I'm sorry. Sally, I'm sorry.

Sally I miss him.

Barbara You loved him, I know.

Sally I'm lonely.

Barbara It'll pass, Sally. It passes.

Sally I've been alone my whole bloody life.

Barbara Me too. And never a sodding moment to myself. Love's not a safe haven, it's a choppy bleedin' ocean. And 'I love you' 's not a lightship, it's a distress signal. Come on.

Sally *shakes her head.*

Barbara You can't stay here.

Sally I want to stay here.

Barbara He's gone, Sally. I was lying in bed the other night and I was cuddling my pillow. Silly sod, but I do. And I heard myself whisper: 'You'll never leave me. You'll always be here.' And I realised I wasn't talking to my pillow, I was talking to myself. And I realised something really obvious, something I've always known but never quite acknowledged. There are two of me. There's the me that needs looking after and there's the me that looks after me. And they've both been there since the very beginning. And the one who looks after me is always going to be there. So whatever happens I'll always have myself, and I'm bleeding good company.

Sally *laughs.*

Barbara   We were laughing.

Sally   What?

Barbara   Kenny asked what the point was. Just before he felt the pain. Well, we were laughing. Come on. Come on. There's a small steakhouse in Stanmore where the owner, if she's in the mood, will ply the clientele with so much free booze you can get way beyond depressed; you can get to fuck it all and the horse it rode in on.

Sally   I can't really drink, I feel really bad next day.

Barbara   That's because you haven't discovered the cure.

Sally   What's the cure?

Barbara   Brent Cross. Come on.

Sally   What if the owner's not in the mood?

Barbara   Don't worry sweetheart; she is.

Barbara *leaves.* **Sally** *turns to follow her and* **Sid** *appears. A tune begins; 'For All We Know'.* **Sally** *hesitates, taking in his shambling posture, his familiar grin. Then she leaves, abruptly.* **Sid** *goes to the table, gathers the pack and shuffles. Out of the shadows comes* **Imogen***. He smiles, she smiles, and she joins him. He deals the cards and they pick up their hands.* **Imogen** *stakes her watch.* **Sid** *stakes his watch. They look at their cards.* **Imogen** *smiles, takes off her top and puts it on the table. The lights fade.*

End.

Printed in the USA
CPSIA information can be obtained
at www.ICGtesting.com
LVHW041059171024
794057LV00001B/162